T0312402

THE ATLAS OF MICROSTATES

Published by Collins
An imprint of HarperCollins Publishers
Westerhill Road, Bishopbriggs, Glasgow G64 2QT
www.harpercollins.co.uk

HarperCollins Publishers
Macken House, 39/40 Mayor Street Upper, Dublin 1, D01 C9W8, Ireland

First edition 2024
© HarperCollins Publishers 2024
Text © Zoran Nikolić 2024
Maps and photographs © see Acknowledgements on page 240

A catalogue record for this book is available from the British Library.

ISBN 978-0-00-870349-3

10 9 8 7 6 5 4 3 2 1

Printed in Bosnia and Herzegovina

If you would like to comment on any aspect of this book,
please contact us at the above address or online.
e-mail: collins.reference@harpercollins.co.uk

collins.co.uk

This book contains FSC™ certified paper and other controlled
sources to ensure responsible forest management.

For more information visit: www.harpercollins.co.uk/green

THE ATLAS OF MICROSTATES

ZORAN NIKOLIĆ

Contents

OVERLEAF: *Satellite view of Vatican City.*
The extent of the microstate has been outlined.

Introduction

Looking at a physical map of the world reveals the magnificent diversity of our planet. The Earth is a place of beautiful mountains, covered with green vegetation and embellished with white, snow-capped peaks. Alongside, you can see mighty rivers, full of precious water and diverse life forms, while just a little further away the picture is entirely different – vast deserts, where the wind shapes new and demolishes old dunes every day. Oceans and seas, the cradles of life on Earth, occupy more than two thirds of the planet's surface and provide a home for the most amazing forms of animals and plants.

However, what happens when we look at a political map of the Earth? Normally we would see different-coloured shapes, which represent numerous sovereign (and somewhat less sovereign) areas. We would see that some of these countries are huge, occupying multiple time zones, while some are so small that you could walk across them in just a day or two. We would see a large number of lines, which show us where the borders are, how much of something is 'ours', and where 'theirs' begins.

What if we could use a time machine to send some sort of satellite mapping device into the past? Would a person in the present day recognise a physical map of the Earth from 100, 500 or 1,000 years ago? Certainly! Maybe there would be more forests in some parts of the planet or maybe some current cities would not exist, but in general, everything would be very similar to today.

On the other hand, if that satellite had the ability to record country borders, or the political map of the world, the situation would be significantly different. Today's political map would be quite different from the one 100 years ago. The one 500 years ago would be vastly different, and the one from 1,000 years ago would be completely unrecognisable to anyone who doesn't have vast historical knowledge at their fingertips. Some areas may show one large country from years ago, where now there are many. Other areas may look like a jigsaw of mini countries, while today they come under one name. When a country is formed, no one can say what its 'best before' or 'expiry' date is. A country, regardless of its size, can last for a very long time, while its neighbour could rapidly disintegrate into smaller states or be absorbed into a larger one.

This book documents some of the smallest countries in the world, some of which may have existed fleetingly, and others that have stood the test of time. We will try to briefly understand how and why those microstates appeared, and why they disappeared. We will also look into the characteristics of each of them, how they dealt with social and natural changes, and also what kind of legacy the now-defunct countries left behind.

Microstates and micronations

The term 'state' is not easy to precisely define. Several conditions need to be met for a territory to be considered a state, and still, not everyone will agree that it is a state. Some of the conditions that a country needs to fulfill in order to earn this title are:

- a clearly defined territory within precisely defined boundaries. (Precision is often difficult to achieve, due to various factors – natural or man-made).
- a clearly defined authority, which establishes, maintains and protects the social order. As in the case of a territory, various factors can hinder the actions of the authorities over the state.
- a high level of sovereignty, which enables independent realisation of the desired relationships with other countries. (Some states are partially sovereign, for example parts of federations, various types of protectorates, etc.)
- the population consists of people living within the territory of the state, and they have citizenship of that state.
- recognition of the state by other states and international organisations. This is a very important condition for the existence and functioning of a state. A state can exist with or without partial recognition of its independence, and on the other hand, the recognition of the independence of a country does not necessarily mean that that country is truly sovereign in the proclaimed territory, or even that it really exists at all. An example of this is a government in exile, which formally represents a state that no longer exists.

The states that are discussed in this book have fulfilled at least some of these conditions, with the additional obligation of being a state territory small enough to be defined as a microstate.

In this book, a microstate is considered to be (at least partially) a sovereign state, which holds its power within a small territory. A small territory is considered to be an area of around, or less than, 2,500 square kilometres.

It should be taken into account that data concerning countries that no longer exist are, almost as a rule, imprecise, and should be taken as a rough estimate. This is especially true for states from ancient times, when borders were not always clearly defined and censuses, if they were kept at all, were often inaccurate.

It is important to note that microstates and micronations are not the same thing. Microstates are essentially true states, with all or most of the attributes of statehood, while micronations are more informal, where without legal basis someone can declare a piece of land, or even someone's apartment, to be an independent state. No micronation has ever been recognised by any official state.

Glossary

Creole language – a language created by mixing several languages. Over time, it becomes the main spoken language of an area, with the language being passed on to new generations.

copra – the dried fleshy part of the coconut. It is used for the production of soap, food, lubricants, etc.

federation – a political union of at least two partially sovereign member states, which have transferred part of their sovereignty to a joint federal state.

marae – in Polynesia it represents a flat, open space for worship and a ceremonial place; a place intended to communicate with the gods and deceased ancestors.

personal union – a political agreement in which one person becomes the monarch of two sovereign states, while the independence of those states is retained.

protectorate – an autonomous state under the protection of another, stronger and usually larger state. A protected state usually retains full internal freedom and governance.

puppet state – a state that is formally independent but is, usually against its will, de facto under the complete military, economic and political control of another state.

vassal state – a state in a subordinate, suppliant or dependent position relative to another state.

About the author

I was born in 1975 in Serbia, which at that time was part of Yugoslavia. Today I live in Austria, where I wrote this book.

Although I am an IT engineer by education, I have forever been interested in geographical maps and atlases, which were always a must on my desk. A thorough study of numerous geographical maps led me to understand the injustices towards countries with a small area of territory. Most of these small countries are not clearly shown, and are often not even visible on maps of the world or of continents. *The Atlas of Microstates* is designed to be a small contribution to correcting that injustice, giving readers the opportunity to get to know the numerous microstates of the modern era, and some from earlier times.

Key to maps

Microstate area/point	
SAMOS □	Microstate capital
İzmir ○	Other town or city
Casino ●	Place of interest
Elba	Physical feature
Snaefell ▲ *625*	Summit (height in metres)
ITALY	Country name
Lazio	Administrative area
───────	International boundary
─ ─ ─ ─	Disputed international boundary
───────	Administrative boundary
·············	Ceasefire line
LATVIA	Historical area name
━━━━━━━	Historical boundary
───────	River
	Lake or sea

EUROPE

Xlendi Tower, dating from 1650, is the oldest of the four surviving watchtowers on Gozo, Malta. Salt pans, designed to extract sea salt, can be seen in the foreground.

PRINCIPALITY OF
ANDORRA

Catalan idyll

LOCATION: Pyrenees
PERIOD: since 1278
AREA: 465 sq km
POPULATION: 79,824

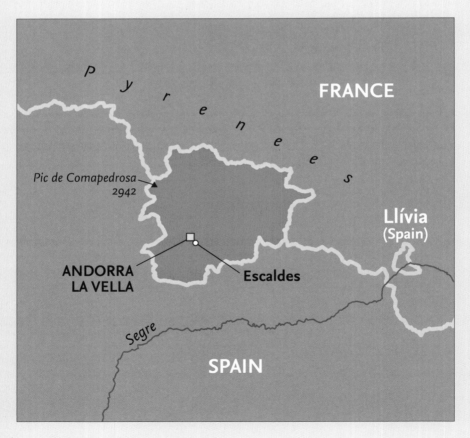

One way of categorising all countries in the world is into republics and monarchies. Put simply, a republic is a form of state government where non-hereditary authorities are elected in free elections (though this isn't always the case), while in a monarchy, power is inherited usually within a single family. But there is also Andorra!

Andorra is a small country (ranking among the top 20 smallest worldwide, both in terms of area and population), situated high in the Pyrenees mountains, on the border between **France** and **Spain**. Andorra's political system is unique and closely tied to its two powerful neighbours. Through a series of historical events, Andorra was defined as a principality, jointly and equally ruled by two co-princes – the ruler of France and the bishop of the Catholic Diocese of Urgell in Spain. This means that one formal ruler of Andorra is elected by the citizens of the neighbouring **French Republic** in free elections, while the other is appointed by the Roman Catholic Church, whose headquarters are in the smallest independent mini-state, the **Vatican**. However, real political power lies with the government and the General Council, the parliament of Andorra, founded as far back as 1419. The Principality is not a member of the **European Union (EU)**, but has signed numerous agreements with the EU, including the possibility of minting its own euro coins.

Despite its very small territory, Andorra today is an extremely popular tourist destination, attracting around 10 million tourists annually. Unsurprisingly, tourism and related activities make up about 80 per cent of the gross domestic product of this tiny country. With numerous ski slopes, a significant amount of snow, an average of 300 sunny days per year, along with one of the largest spa centres in the world, Andorra is a very attractive holiday destination for the French and Spanish, as well as those from further afield. It has a wealth of high mountains (the highest peak is 2,942 metres), and the capital, Andorra La Vella, is located at 1,023 metres above sea level, earning it the title of the highest European capital. Interestingly, the lowest point of Andorra is at an impressive 840 metres. This healthy and clean environment is one of the main reasons for the exceptional longevity of the local population. The fact that Andorra is nestled high in the Pyrenees, between two powerful neighbours, means that the small principality, the only independent country in the world where Catalan is the official language, has never had a standing army or a Ministry of Defence. In fact, Andorra has not participated in any military conflicts for centuries.

Legend has it that the Catalans from today's Andorra helped the mighty Frankish Emperor Charlemagne in the battles against the **Emirate of Córdoba**. In gratitude, Charlemagne granted privileges to the local population, which was considered the first step in the founding of the modern Principality of Andorra. This is also celebrated in the lyrics of Andorra's national anthem:

I was born a princess and heiress between two nations, neutral;
I am the only remaining daughter of the Carolingian empire.

FREE STATE OF
BOTTLENECK

Smuggler zone in Rhineland

LOCATION: present-day Hesse and
Rhineland-Palatinate, Germany

PERIOD: 1919–1923

AREA: c. 150 sq km

POPULATION: c. 17,000

The end of the First World War led to a temporary occupation of the Rhineland, a region in Germany west of the River Rhine, extending to the borders with **France**, **Luxembourg**, **Belgium**, and the **Netherlands**. The Entente Powers (France, **Britain** and the **United States**) occupied and demilitarised this area, creating a kind of buffer zone towards France and Belgium. To strengthen the Allied positions in the Rhineland, three bridgeheads were formed – semi-circular military positions with a radius of 30 kilometres centred in Cologne (British zone), Koblenz (American zone), and Mainz (French zone).

From this moment, the story of the Free State of Bottleneck begins. When drawing the boundary of the bridgeheads on the eastern bank of the Rhine, military cartographers overlooked the fact that a narrow area remained between the French and American zones. This area was separated from the rest of Germany by the exceptionally challenging terrain of the Taunus mountains, and therefore without any roads and railways. At the same time, all crossings between this elongated region and the adjacent bridgeheads were closed, and ships on the Rhine were not allowed to dock in the towns of Kaub and Lorch. In this way, in 1919, a territory was formed that formally remained under German control, but where **Germany** could not enforce its laws. The shape of this semi-independent territory resembled a bottleneck, earning it its unofficial name.

The residents of this unusual area, numbering between 8,000 and 17,000 depending on the source, quickly realised that they would have to organise themselves to survive and prosper. So, it was decided that Edmund Pnischeck, the mayor of Lorch, the largest town in the region, would become the president of Bottleneck. He remained in this position throughout the existence of this de facto mini-state. Life in Bottleneck was certainly not simple. Not only was there a shortage of everything as a consequence of the First World War, but Bottleneck was also almost completely isolated from all sides. This forced many residents of the Free State to engage in smuggling. There was even a recorded case of the local population kidnapping an entire train transporting coal to the French mines in the occupied part of Germany. The coal was then distributed to all residents to help them survive the harsh winter. Despite the challenging conditions, Bottleneck even printed its own postage stamps (although letters had to be smuggled too!) and money, and passport issuance was also initiated.

As Germany failed to fulfil its obligations under the peace treaty with the Allies, France decided to temporarily occupy the entire Rhineland region in 1923. This military endeavour was used as an opportunity to annex the entire area of the Free State of Bottleneck into the French occupation zone. A few years later, after the French withdrew, the region was incorporated into the Prussian province of Hesse-Nassau. Today, the name Bottleneck is used as a tourist attraction in that part of the Upper Middle Rhine Valley UNESCO World Heritage Site.

GREEK COMMUNITY OF
BULKES

From abandoned village to city-state

LOCATION: present-day Serbia
PERIOD: 1945–1949
AREA: less than 10 sq km
POPULATION: C. 5,000

Anyone familiar with the basics of ancient Greek history is certainly familiar with the term 'polis'. These were ancient city-states scattered all over the region of the former ancient Greek civilization, which disappeared over time, eventually merging into present-day **Greece**.

Hundreds of years later, after the Second World War, a small polis suddenly arose in an unexpected area, on the southern edges of the fertile Pannonian Plain, not far from **Novi Sad**, the capital of the Serbian Autonomous Province of Vojvodina.

Although this seems unusual and unexpected, the 'how and why' is relatively simple. Immediately after the end of the Second World War, a civil war between the government's monarchist and communist forces started in liberated Greece. Despite the initial success, the communist forces soon began to suffer losses, so a large number of this group's members found asylum in neighbouring communist **Yugoslavia**. In the fertile plains of Vojvodina, the Yugoslav authorities let them have a deserted German village named Bulkes. The village was abandoned due to virtually all Germans being expelled from the former Austro-Hungarian Danube region after the Second World War. This temporary refugee camp soon became an autonomous Greek municipality, with many characteristics of a real state. Bulkes was given clearly defined borders, and entry and exit from the polis was controlled by the Yugoslav and internal Greek police. As a means of payment, the so-called Bulkes dinar was used, on which *ΕΛΛΗΝΙΚΗ ΚΟΙΝΟΤΗΤΑ ΜΠΩΥΛΚΕΣ* (Greek Community of Bulkes) was printed. These banknotes were legally printed in the Greek community, and the Yugoslav authorities permitted their use in the territory of this mini-state.

The population of Bulkes ranged from 3,000 to 6,000 people. There were Greek schools, a theatre, a library, a hospital in the village and school textbooks and newspapers were printed in Greek, like 'The Voice of Bulkes' – *Φωνη του Μπουλκες*. The badge of the communist Democratic Army of Greece was used as a coat of arms – shown on the opposite page, it is a blue circle with a red Greek letter Delta (this stands for *Δημοκρατία*, meaning both "democracy" and "republic" in Greek). In 1948 there was a big conflict between Yugoslavia and other communist countries, primarily the Soviet Union (USSR). As the Greek communists from Bulkes then aligned with the USSR, Yugoslavia decided to immediately dissolve the Greek community, and the majority of the inhabitants found a new home in the then **Czechoslovakia** (now two separate countries: Czechia and Slovakia) and other countries, by choice or force. As soon as the majority had left Bulkes, the village was named Maglić – and new inhabitants settled there, Serbian colonists from **Bosnia and Herzegovina**. Today, there are hardly any traces of the former Greek state in northern **Serbia**, except for a few monuments in the local cemetery.

CHANNEL ISLANDS:
BAILIWICK OF JERSEY AND
BAILIWICK OF GUERNSEY

*The last remnants of
the Duchy of Normandy*

LOCATION: English Channel
PERIOD: since 1204
AREA: Jersey 116 sq km
    Guernsey 78 sq km
POPULATION: Jersey 110,778; Guernsey 63,301

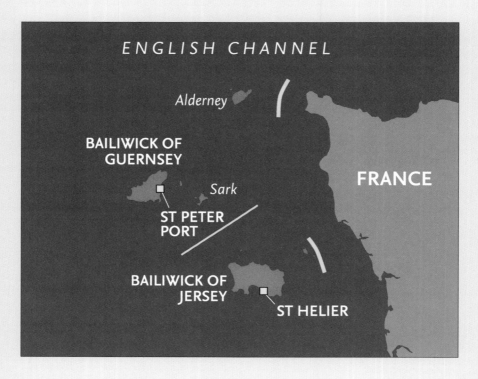

After the successful invasion of England in 1066, the Norman Duke William II became the new King of England, best known as William the Conqueror, thus uniting **Normandy** and **England** under one crown. Two centuries later, the French King Philip II managed to conquer almost all of England's estates in **France**, except for a few small islands in the English Channel. With the Paris Peace Treaty of 1259, these islands, known as the Channel Islands, officially were still in the hands of the English Crown.

Today, the term Channel Islands encompasses the last remnants of the Duchy of Normandy – the **Bailiwick** of Jersey and the Bailiwick of Guernsey – two separate political entities that have never been part of England or the United Kingdom. The governance over these islands rests with the King or Queen of the United Kingdom, while the 'Bailiffs' are the civic heads and the presidents of the Royal Court. These are not the bailiffs of the debt-collecting capacity, but titles bestowed on those in the highest judicial offices in Jersey and Guernsey. The monarch of the United Kingdom is still known on the islands by the informal title 'Duke of Normandy'.

Jersey is larger in both area and population than Guernsey, though the latter consists of three politically separate territories: Guernsey itself (including Herm), along with the neighbouring islands of Alderney and Sark. This complex system is a result of the preservation of certain feudal peculiarities of the medieval Duchy of Normandy. In fact, many considered the island of Sark to be the last feudal state, until 2008 when the first free elections were held on the island.

Until 1948, French was the only official language in both Bailiwicks, while a small number of inhabitants spoke English and the local Norman dialects – Dgèrnésiais in Guernsey and Jèrriais in Jersey. Today, the situation is significantly different: English has become the official language, regularly spoken by more than 80% of the inhabitants of the Channel Islands. French remains a language of administration but only a few hundred people use it as their first language, and it is similar numbers for speakers of local Norman dialects.

The islands are known for their natural beauty, unique wildlife, mild maritime climate, as well as for the production and export of fruits, flowers, potatoes, and tomatoes. Many artists and writers have spent time on the Channel Islands, among them Victor Hugo, who wrote the last part of his masterpiece *Les Misérables* there. His novel *Les Travailleurs de la Mer* (The Toilers of the Sea) takes place in Guernsey.

For all those afraid of witches, Jersey and Guernsey are quite safe places. Many houses on these islands have witches' seats (or witches' stones), thin stone slabs protruding from the chimneys. Their purpose is to provide witches, tired from flying on their broomsticks, a place to sit and have a rest. If a house doesn't have this seat, witches could get seriously upset, and nobody wants that. (The scientific explanation is that these slabs were meant to prevent water from leaking down the chimney, but that doesn't sound as interesting.)

REPUBLIC OF
COSPAIA

'Perpetual freedom' and tobacco

LOCATION: Umbria–Tuscany border, Italy
PERIOD: 1440–1826
AREA: 3.3 sq km
POPULATION: C. 500

In the mid-15th century, when Pope Eugene IV allowed the **Republic of Florence** to take control of the town of Sansepolcro in central **Italy**, it was necessary to establish a new border between the Papal States and Florence. It was agreed that this border should follow the course of a small river known as the Rio, a minor tributary of the mighty Tiber. However, this is where the problem arose: there were two streams that flowed almost parallel to each other and both flowed into the Tiber, practically side by side. Since neither the Pope nor the Florentines were inclined to argue (as disputes at that time almost always led to swords and bloodshed), they simply said that they were not interested in that small strip of land, so they established their borders along the stream that was closer to them. Thus, Florence set its border along the stream now known as Gorgaccia, while the border of the Papal States was established along the stream now called Riascone.

When the inhabitants of the small village of Cospaia, situated between the two aforementioned streams, realised that they had suddenly become terra nullius (no man's land), they decided to immediately declare independence. And so, the independent Republic of Cospaia (Republica de' Cošpäja in the local dialect), was proclaimed in the year 1440 on these 3.3 square kilometres of free territory. Now comes the most peculiar fact: this miniature republic, with around 500 inhabitants, survived for almost four centuries. During this time, the microstate prospered continuously, much like its larger neighbours, the Papal States and the Republic of Florence (later the **Grand Duchy of Tuscany**).

What distinguished Cospaia from other states, apart from its size, was its unusual organisation which encouraged the complete freedom of all inhabitants, similar to a commune. The republic did not have a traditional government, taxes, prisons, a military, or even a police force. The only law was *Perpetua et firma libertas* ('Perpetual and secure freedom'). The supreme governing body was the Council of Elders and Family Heads, comprising representatives from all families, and responsible for making decisions related to the economy and security of Cospaia. The secret to Cospaia's success was that it was the only territory on the **Apennine Peninsula** where free cultivation of tobacco was allowed, making this plant the main source of income for the miniature republic.

This happy story began to crumble at the beginning of the 19th century when various criminals sought refuge in the small anarchist republic. Pressured by the Pope and the Grand Duke of Tuscany, representatives of the Republic of Cospaia decided to become part of the Papal State in 1826 but with permission to continue cultivating tobacco. At the entrance to the small town of Cospaia, a welcome sign to the former free mini-republic still stands today.

COUTO MISTO

Galician fairytale

LOCATION: Spain–Portugal border
PERIOD: 1100s–1864
AREA: 27 sq km
POPULATION: C. 1,000

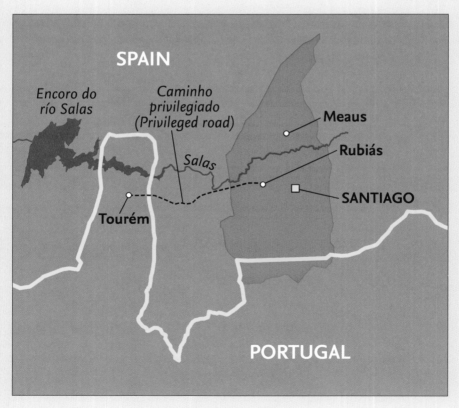

Once upon a time there was a princess. Although she was pregnant, under the pressure of her enemies, she had to leave the safety of her palace and flee to the remote parts of her country. During her journey she gave birth, and the peasants from three nearby villages selflessly helped her. Later, when she returned to power, the princess showed her gratitude by granting special rights to the residents of those three villages, creating a de facto semi-independent state.

Even though this seems like the beginning of a fairy tale, this is actually one (possible) tale about how this tiny and almost unknown state on the border of present-day **Portugal** and **Spain** – Couto Misto – was created. If this story is true, and many believe it is, Couto Misto was established in the 12th century, when the inhabitants of the villages of Santiago, Rubiás and Meaus in the Salas river valley were given some sort of autonomy and independence from the surrounding noblemen, as well as from the kingdoms of Portugal and Spain, which at that time had just begun to emerge. As time went by, the Portuguese and Spanish rulers realised that there was not much use in fighting over such a small piece of land, so Couto Misto maintained its independence for several hundred years. This lasted until the second half of the 19th century, when Spain and Portugal finally decided to clearly define their borders. At that time Spain took over all three villages, while Portugal settled for a small uninhabited area in the south of Couto Misto, as well as some small areas along other parts of the border with **Galicia**. Of course, no one asked the residents of 'Galician Andorra' for their opinion on the new borders. (Note: Galicia is an autonomous community in northwestern Spain, north of Portugal; the inhabitants of this region speak Galician – called 'Galego' in Galician – to a large extent, which is a sister language of Portuguese.)

During Couto Misto's approximately seven centuries of existence, its inhabitants had some specific rights: they did not pay taxes to the local noblemen, nor to the Portuguese or Spanish crowns; they could choose their nationality, namely whether they wanted to be defined as Portuguese, Spanish, both or neither. They were not obliged to serve in the army, but they were allowed to carry their personal weapons at all times. They were allowed to grow any agricultural crops, and often it was tobacco, which in Portugal and Spain was under strict state monopoly. Couto Misto had some sort of democratic government, headed by an elected *Juiz* (Civil and Governing Judge), who was helped by three assistants, one from each village. One unusual right enjoyed by the residents of this microstate was the so-called *Caminho privilegiado* ('Privileged road'), which the inhabitants of Couto Misto used to transport their goods to the nearby Portuguese town of **Tourém**, without ever being stopped by the authorities.

Today Couto Misto (Portuguese: Couto Misto; Galician: Couto Mixto; Spanish: Coto Mixto) does not have any political status, but some individuals and local politicians are trying to mark the existence of this former microstate in some way.

FREE CITY OF
CRACOW

Free, independent, and strictly neutral city

LOCATION: Southern Poland
PERIOD: 1815–1846
AREA: 1,164 sq km
POPULATION: C. 95,000–150,000

0   30 km

The military defeat of Napoleon and the collapse of his **French Empire**, which, with its allies, had control of almost all of Western, Central, and Southern Europe, led to the Congress of Vienna in 1815. At this gathering, the great powers decided how to divide up these territories. One such territory was the French puppet state, the Duchy of Warsaw, also known as Napoleonic **Poland**, which was divided between the Russian Empire and the Kingdom of Prussia, with the support of the Austrian Empire. However, the southernmost part of the Warsaw Duchy became a separate microstate, encompassing the city of Cracow (called Kraków in Polish) and its surroundings.

Although small, this state had a grand and impressive official name: Free, Independent, and Strictly Neutral City of Cracow with its Territory. More commonly known as the Free City of Cracow, it was a condominium, meaning a territory under the joint control of its mega-powerful neighbours, **Russia**, **Prussia**, and **Austria**. Nevertheless, it mainly functioned as an independent state, and developed rapidly economically due to free trade and low taxes. The state was governed by a parliament known as the Assembly of Representatives, and a government, the Governing Senate – all under the supervision of commissars of the partitioning powers.

Nearly 150,000 people lived in this area of approximately 1,200 square kilometres, predominantly Catholics (85%) and Jews (14%). In addition to the city of Cracow itself, the microstate included about 200 surrounding villages and several smaller towns.

The Free City of Cracow was the first (somewhat) independent Polish state since the Third Partition of Poland at the end of the 18th century. However, this freedom, as well as the highly reputable Jagiellonian University, attracted numerous nationally oriented Poles, which was not at all pleasing to its neighbours, especially Austria. That is why, in 1833, after the unsuccessful November Uprising in **Warsaw** and the rest of the semi-autonomous Russian Poland, the three powers decided to reduce the powers of Cracow's senators and representatives while increasing the authority of their delegates. Soon after that, the police force of the Free City was disbanded, replaced by Austrian police.

The end of the Free City of Cracow came in 1846 when the Kraków Uprising (in Cracow), aimed at liberating all of Poland, failed. Austria reacted severely, occupying the city and immediately annexing it into the Empire as the Grand Duchy of **Kraków**, while the Austrian Emperor added the title of the Grand Duke of Kraków to his name. The Poles had to wait for the next 70 years to gain their independent state, finally achieving it in 1918 after the end of the First World War.

FREE CITY OF
DANZIG

A desirable port

LOCATION: Polish Baltic coast
PERIOD: 1920–1939
AREA: 1,950 sq km
POPULATION: 360,000

0   40 km

The end of the First World War led to the redrawing of numerous state borders. Some states grew, some shrank, some disappeared, and some new ones emerged on the geographical map.

One of the new-old states was Poland, which had not existed as an independent state since the end of the 18th century when Russia, Prussia, and Austria divided the Polish lands among themselves (briefly, the Free City of Cracow existed as a miniature Polish state). The rebirth of **Poland** meant that **Germany** would have to cede a significant area to its new eastern neighbour. Naturally, Poland also wanted access to the sea, so it asked the Allies for the city formerly known in German as Danzig (Polish: **Gdańsk**), a major port on the Baltic Sea. Germany strongly opposed this, and it had an unexpected ally in **Britain**. The British government believed that taking Danzig from Germany and giving it to Poland would provoke such anger in the Reich that it would only be a matter of time before a new conflict erupted.

The Treaty of Versailles in 1919 led to a compromise solution: Poland was granted a narrow 'Polish Corridor' to the **Baltic coast**, and Danzig was separated from Germany but not handed over to the Poles – instead, it was declared a Free City. It was an almost independent territory, under the authority of the League of Nations (predecessor of the United Nations) but in a customs, railway, and postal union with Poland. Poland also represented the City's interests abroad and had special rights to use the city port.

The creation of the Free City of Danzig was not a perfect solution. The majority (about 90%) of the population in the area were of German ethnic origin, and opposed separation from Germany. This constant dissatisfaction led to the growing popularity of the Nazi Party, culminating in an absolute victory in the 1933 elections, when they won the majority of seats in the Volkstag – the parliament of Danzig. The consequence was the suppression of freedom of speech and arrests based on political or national affiliation, all of which served as a prelude to the devastating Second World War. The day Germany invaded Poland, Danzig was 'absorbed' into the **Third Reich**. After the war, it was annexed to Poland, and the German inhabitants were largely expelled to their homeland. Interestingly, for several years at the beginning of the 19th century, Danzig was also known as the Free City, but as an autonomous city-state within the **Napoleonic Empire**.

A large number of notable persons originated from the Free City of Danzig, for example, the renowned German actor Klaus Kinski, as well as the famous writer and Nobel Prize laureate Günter Grass, who emphasised multiple times that he ethnically identified as a member of the Kashubian people. The Kashubians (Kashubian: Kaszëbi) are a small West Slavic ethnic group, closely related to the Poles. It is believed that Kashubians and an even smaller group, the Slovincians, are direct descendants of the former Slavic tribe of Pomeranians. Today, they predominantly inhabit the area of Gdańsk, the nearby city of Gdynia, and the aforementioned 'Polish Corridor'.

DEBATABLE LANDS

The English–Scottish border is here... somewhere

LOCATION: England–Scotland border
PERIOD: 1100s–1552
AREA: c. 100 sq km
POPULATION: a few thousand

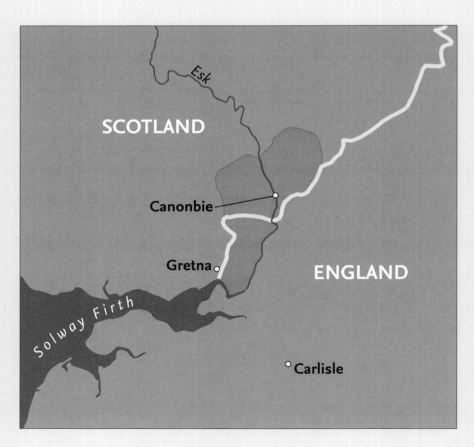

When the English King Henry III and the Scottish King Alexander II signed the Treaty of York in 1237, establishing the first English–Scottish border, few thought that it would last. Nevertheless, it has remained almost unchanged to this day. The only noticeable changes to date have been at the easternmost and westernmost points of the border. At the easternmost point, the English and Scottish flags have both been flown from the town walls of Berwick-upon-Tweed. At the westernmost point lay an area with an unusual name: the Debatable Lands.

The Debatable Lands represent a small area around the lower course of the River Esk as far as its confluence with the Solway Firth. A large part of this area consisted of permanent marshes and peat bogs, posing a challenge for both English and Scottish authorities to control. This was taken advantage of by numerous powerful clans living within the Debatable Lands, with perhaps the most notable being the Armstrong clan, whose coat of arms is shown on the previous page (the most famous descendant of this clan was Neil Armstrong, the first person to walk on the Moon). Members of these clans would steal livestock from farms on both the Scottish and English sides of the border, returning with their loot to the safety of their hideouts around the Esk. Over time, this territory evolved into a kind of unofficial state where neither England nor Scotland had any authority for a full 300 years! In actual fact, the Debatable Lands were never officially declared a free, sovereign state, but the reality on the ground resembled the early stages of a new, small, anarchist entity with relatively clear borders. Within the territory, sometimes known as **Threpe** (Scots term: 'to argue'), several villages existed, with the largest being **Canonbie** (Scottish Gaelic: Canonbaidh).

It took more than 300 years for the English and Scottish monarchs to put an end once and for all to the plundering raids of the powerful clans in the Debatable Lands. Before the final agreement, both Scottish and English palaces had jointly allowed all Scots and English to rob or kill anyone from the Debatable Lands without any legal consequences. With the support of the French ambassador, an agreement was signed in 1552, finally putting an end to this small, lawless region – on paper. The Debatable Lands are divided on the geographical map by an almost straight line, which on the ground transforms into Scots' Dike, a 5.5-kilometre-long embankment, representing the final part of the now well-defined England–Scotland border. However, more than 50 years had to pass until the crowns of Scotland and England were united by James VI and I, King of England, Scotland, and Ireland. Only then did the right time come for a successful fight against lawlessness in the Debatable Lands – in practice.

PRINCIPALITY OF
ELBA

Napoleon's first island of exile

LOCATION: between Italy and Corsica
PERIOD: 1814–1815
AREA: 224 sq km
POPULATION: 12,000

At the beginning of the 19th century, for several years, Napoleon Bonaparte ruled over one of the largest European states of all time, when the French Empire, along with its puppet states and allies, had control over most of Europe. However, in 1814, the so-called War of the Sixth Coalition ended when the alliance of **Austria**, **Russia**, **Prussia**, **Britain**, **Spain**, and **Sweden** defeated the French Empire. With the Treaty of Fontainebleau, Napoleon abdicated, and the allied powers granted him the small Mediterranean island of Elba as an independent and non-hereditary duchy and as his personal property. According to the treaty, Napoleon could rule over Elba for the rest of his life, after which the island would be returned to the Grand Duchy of **Tuscany**. The island is situated between **Corsica** and **Italy**, only 15 kilometres off the Tuscan coast, and measuring 20 kilometres by 10 kilometres.

Not having much of a choice, Napoleon accepted the Duchy of Elba, where he landed on 4 May 1814. According to the treaty, he took several dozen sailors and about 1,000 soldiers with him. He began to organise and modernise his island: improving the operation of local mines, initiating the construction of a hospital, water supply system, roads, and bridges, introducing new laws, organising a fire brigade and establishing a new government for the duchy.

Napoleon's wife decided not to join her husband on Elba, so the members of the Sixth Coalition assigned her the small Italian state of the Duchy of **Parma** and Piacenza, where she ruled for the rest of her life. On the other hand, Napoleon's sister Pauline came to his small duchy. Prior to that, she had sold all her property in France to help her brother in exile. Pauline's arrival brought with it theatre performances, receptions, and balls.

It is interesting that the French poet and novelist Victor Hugo briefly lived on Elba as a boy, as his father was an officer in the army of Napoleon's duchy. The majority of the microstate's income was spent on the army, which was derived from taxes on mines, salt, fishing, and also by money paid by France. Though the Elbanis were initially pleased with the arrival of an emperor to their small island, they rebelled when Napoleon was forced to raise taxes after France withdrew financial support.

This would likely have led to serious problems for Napoleon had he not decided to return to France just ten months after his forced arrival on Elba. There, he attempted to regain his imperial throne but was defeated after the Hundred Days, the term coined for the period of his brief return to power. He was then exiled to St Helena, a remote British island in the South Atlantic. This time, it was the final defeat for Napoleon, the descendant of an Italian noble family from Corsica, a powerful general, the First Consul of the French Republic, Emperor of the French, and absolute ruler of the Duchy of Elba.

Portoferraio, the capital of Elba. Napoleon's Palace, today a museum dedicated to the sole ruler of the Duchy of Elba, is located on the east side of the fortified town.

The Governor's Palace in Fiume (modern-day Rijeka) was the seat of Riccardo Zanella's government. Today, it is the Maritime and History Museum of the Croatian Littoral, and the square in front of this Renaissance-style building is named after the only president of the Free State of Fiume.

FREE STATE OF
FIUME

Fascism's first foothold

LOCATION: coast of present-day Croatia
PERIOD: 1920–1924
AREA: 28 sq km
POPULATION: 50,000

CROATIA
(present-day)

ITALY

YUGOSLAVIA

Rječina

FIUME

ADRIATIC SEA

0   5 km

The foundations of the **Austro-Hungarian Empire** had been unstable for quite some time, but its defeat in the First World War led to the complete collapse and the dissolution of this Central European power. New states emerged where the once-mighty empire was, while some lands were seized by neighbouring countries. One small part of the Austro-Hungarian Empire was the city of Fiume (modern-day Rijeka), on the northern shores of the Adriatic Sea. This significant port was desired by both the Kingdom of Italy and the newly formed Kingdom of Serbs, Croats, and Slovenes (created by the unification of the Kingdom of **Serbia** and Austro-Hungarian territories inhabited by South Slavic populations; later named the Kingdom of Yugoslavia).

When the victorious Great Powers of the First World War (Britain, France, and the United States) realised that Italy and **Yugoslavia** would not easily come to an agreement on the status of Fiume, they decided to create an independent city-state. The establishment of this independent microstate did not go smoothly, and it was further complicated by the Italian poet and general Gabriele d'Annunzio, a founder of Italian fascism. With a few hundred legionnaires, he seized Fiume and offered it to Italy. However, Italy and Yugoslavia concluded the Rapallo Agreement, which declared Fiume a free state, and d'Annunzio was soon expelled from the city by military force.

The Great Powers' recognition of Fiume's independence made it possible for parliamentary elections to be held as early as 1921. The elections saw a confrontation between the pro-Italian bloc and the autonomists. The autonomists, who advocated Fiume's independence and were against its annexation to Italy, won convincingly. Their leader at the time, Riccardo Zanella, became the first and only president of the Free State. Unfortunately, Zanella and his government did not have time to achieve anything significant, as only six months after the presidential elections, Italian fascists carried out a coup d'état, and overthrew the legally elected government, making the Free State of Fiume the first country to fall into the hands of fascist expansionists. Months later, in March 1922, the newly fascist Italian military would enter the city and restore order.

The following year, Italy and Yugoslavia signed the Treaty of Rome, which put an end to the Free State of Fiume in 1924. The majority of this small state went to Italy, while Yugoslavia took over **Sušak**, the eastern suburb of the city. Zanella and his exiled government lobbied for the re-establishment of this state for a long time, up until the early 1950s. They even had discussions with Josip Broz Tito, the powerful new Yugoslav leader. However, in 1947, Yugoslavia officially annexed Fiume and the Istrian Peninsula and incorporated them into Croatia, one of its federal units.

The Free State of Fiume was a multi-ethnic and multi-religious state. Its official languages were Italian, Hungarian, and German. Additionally, **Venetian** and the so-called Chakavian **Croatian** language, a distinct dialect of the Croatian language with numerous loanwords from Italian and Venetian, were widely spoken. This microstate had no chance of survival because its large neighbours never wished for it to endure.

FREE CITY OF
FRANKFURT

From microstate to financial centre of Europe

LOCATION: present-day Hesse, Germany
PERIOD: 1372–1866
AREA: 50 sq km
POPULATION: 90,000

GERMANY

Frankfurt
am Main

Offenbach
am Main

Wiesbaden

Mainz

Main

Rhine

Darmstadt

0   20 km

For centuries, the German ethnic area was made up of many small states, which were allies one day, and at war with each other the next. One of these small states was the Free City of Frankfurt, which was actually an independent city-state from the late 1300s all the way until the mid-19th century.

In 1372, Frankfurt and its immediate surroundings were declared a Free Imperial City, making it a member of the **Holy Roman Empire** under the direct authority of the emperor, without any feudal lord as an intermediary.

Soon, Frankfurt became an important transport and trade centre, which strengthened the city's financial power. The wealthy Rothschild family, originating from Frankfurt, owned some of the leading European banks, and it is no surprise that emperors of the Holy Roman Empire were crowned in this city. Owing to its prestige, the Free City had diplomatic ties with the **United States**, **Russia**, **Prussia**, **France**, **Britain**, **Austria**, and numerous other states.

The city primarily developed on the north bank of the Main, in a densely populated 2-square-kilometre area, with 40,000 inhabitants in the 1300s, increasing to over 70,000 by the 19th century. On the other side of the river, a new part of Frankfurt, Sachsenhausen, developed with approximately 5,000 inhabitants. In addition to this urban area of about 3 square kilometres, the microstate of Frankfurt also included the Forest District (today, it represents a significant part of the extremely popular Frankfurt City Forest), covering an area of about 40 square kilometres. An additional few square kilometres were made up of several small exclaves.

The appearance of Napoleon on the European stage brought a temporary end to the Free City of Frankfurt, which was enlarged with some surrounding territories and then declared the Grand Duchy of Frankfurt, becoming another one of the numerous French puppet states. Napoleon's fall from power led to the Congress of Vienna in 1815, which, among other things, reinstated the Free City of Frankfurt, this time within the German Confederation, a loose alliance of many, mostly small, states. The Federal Convention, which was the permanent congress of delegates of all member states of the German Confederation, was headquartered in Frankfurt itself.

After the Austro-Prussian War of 1866, Prussia took control of the German states from Austria; the German Confederation was dissolved; and the North German Confederation was formed in its place, only a few years later becoming the **German Empire**. However, one crucial consequence concerned Frankfurt. When the war began, Frankfurt was neutral, which did not please Prussia, who took the view that 'who is not with us is against us'. The Prussian army effortlessly occupied the undefended city on 16 July 1866, while the Austro-Prussian war was still going on. Most democratic freedoms of the Free City were abolished, most newspapers were prohibited and Frankfurt was soon incorporated into the newly formed province of **Hesse-Nassau**.

Today, Frankfurt serves as a major transportation hub in Europe, as well as a financial centre, being the financial capital of Germany and the Eurozone, home to the European Central Bank, the German Federal Bank, and numerous financial institutions.

REPUBLIC OF
GERSAU

The independent Swiss riviera

LOCATION: present-day Switzerland
PERIOD: 1390–1817
AREA: 24 sq km
POPULATION: C. 1,000

0   10 km

A pleasant climate, the beautiful Lake Lucerne, a large number of chestnut trees, and an occasional palm tree makes every summer visitor of the Swiss town of Gersau feel like they are somewhere in the Mediterranean region. Another distinctive aspect of this small town is that for almost four centuries, it was actually an independent microstate. This area was owned by the powerful Habsburg dynasty until the mid-14th century, when it became the property of local nobility from the nearby town of **Lucerne**. In order to protect itself from potential attacks, the town voluntarily became a protectorate of the Old Swiss Confederacy, the precursor to today's **Switzerland**. The most crucial moment for this microstate occurred in 1390 when the inhabitants of Gersau bought themselves, and their village, freedom from the owners in Lucerne. From then, Gersau began to function in every respect as an independent state, officially confirmed in 1433 when Sigismund of Luxembourg, the Holy Roman Emperor, granted it the status of a free imperial city. This meant that only the Emperor was above the local government of the town, and Gersau autonomously managed its internal and external affairs, with the protection of four surrounding cantons. These cantons (Luzern, Schwyz, Uri, and Unterwalden – now Nidwalden and Obwalden) were known as the 'Four Forest Cantons', and from this nickname Lake Lucerne got its German, French, and Italian name, 'Lake of the Four (Forest) Cantons'.

The geographical position also contributed to the independence of Gersau. The town, known as the Riviera of Central Switzerland, is situated on a small, sunny plateau on the shore of Lake Lucerne, but is surrounded by mountains on all other sides, making it isolated like an island. In older times, the majority of the population was engaged in woodworking and silk weaving. Today, Gersau is a significant spa and tourist centre, known for events like the StradivariFEST, where musicians play on the lake, in the local church, on boats, and other unconventional places, using instruments of the renowned Italian master, Antonio Stradivari.

At the very end of the 18th century, Napoleon Bonaparte played a part in the story of the Republic of Gersau. His powerful army had conquered the territory of present-day Switzerland, and established the Helvetic Republic there, a sister republic (in reality, a puppet state) of France. This resulted in the abolition of the independence of Gersau and its annexation to the canton of Schwyz. However, immediately after Napoleon was overthrown from power in 1814, the inhabitants of Gersau once again declared their republic to be independent, with the support of their four neighbouring protector cantons. These final moments of the *Altfrye Republik Gersau* ('Old-Free Republic of Gersau' – the name under which the Swiss microstate was known) were short-lived. Under the agreement of the Congress of Vienna and the Swiss Federal Treaty, Gersau was annexed to the canton of Schwyz in 1817 (though actually only the borders of Schwyz were mentioned). What is interesting is that Gersau was not mentioned in the conclusions of the Congress of Vienna, nor in the Federal Treaty, leading to the conclusion that neither the great powers, nor the majority of the Swiss, were aware of the existence of, or at least the re-emergence of, the Altfrye Republik.

GOZO:
THE GOZITAN NATION

Island of the French, British and Odysseus

LOCATION: present-day Malta
PERIOD: 1798–1801
AREA: 67 sq km
POPULATION: 16,000

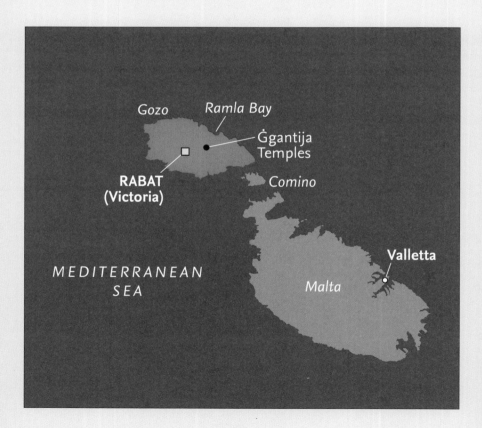

In 1798, when Napoleon Bonaparte set out with a fleet of 30,000 soldiers and sailors to conquer Egypt, he found they needed somewhere to rest and replenish the ships with food. **Malta** seemed like a good choice, so he requested permission to dock from the Knights of Malta, who had ruled this archipelago as feudal lords since the late 13th century. Referring to their neutrality, the Knights allowed only two ships at a time to enter the Maltese ports. Napoleon was not satisfied with this, and he quickly took over the whole of Malta and its surrounding islands through rapid military action.

The Maltese soon rose in rebellion against the French, and the British eagerly came to the aid of the enemies of their enemies. The island of Malta fell into the hands of the British, but the siege of the French garrisons in Valletta and the surrounding towns lasted almost two years.

At the same time, a small French garrison on the neighbouring island of Gozo surrendered at the end of 1798, and the British handed control of the island over to the local population, along with complete French armaments and ammunition. The Gozitans appointed a local priest, Saverio Cassar, as the governor of the island, while King Ferdinand was recognised as the formal ruler (Ferdinand was known as Ferdinand IV, King of Naples; Ferdinand III, King of Sicily; and Ferdinand I after the unification of Sicily and Naples). For the next 1,000 days, the island of Gozo functioned as an independent state – though it received weapons and food from Naples – with its capital in the town of Rabat (officially known today as Victoria), located in the centre of the island. The Gozitan government established a new administration, introduced courts, and attempted to initiate other reforms. The flag of the Kingdom of **Naples** was chosen for the flag of the small island state.

This microstate is often referred to today as The Gozitan Nation (Italian: La Nazione Gozitana; Maltese: In-Nazzjon Għawdxi), to distinguish it from the name of the island itself. Unfortunately, the island's independence was short-lived: in 1801, Britain decided to annex Gozo to its Malta Protectorate, which was still formally part of the **Kingdom of Sicily**, but under British protection.

The island of Gozo is known for its ancient megalithic monuments (the Ġgantija Temples were built over 5,500 years ago), fascinating bays (Inland Sea is a lagoon connected to the sea by a small natural sea tunnel), and the mighty Cittadella, built by the Knights of Malta as a defence against constant attacks from the Ottoman Empire, which offers an unforgettable view of the entire island. On the northeast coast lies Ramla Bay with beaches featuring reddish sand. Right next to this bay is the so-called Calypso's Cave, where, according to legend, the nymph Calypso held Odysseus captive for seven years. Who knows, perhaps even today it is still possible to hear the song of this nymph on the rocky shores of the island of Gozo, as she awaits the return of her beloved Odysseus.

FREE STATE OF
IKARIA

Icarus' resting place

LOCATION: Aegean Sea, present-day Greece
PERIOD: 1912
AREA: 300 sq km
POPULATION: 16,000

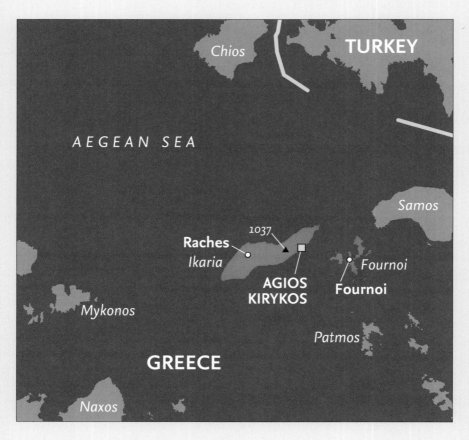

According to legend, when Daedalus and Icarus escaped from the island of Crete using wings made of wax and feathers, young Icarus did not listen to his father's advice to avoid flying too close to the Sun. In an attempt to reach the heights of the gods and prove he was equal to them, Icarus flew too high, causing his waxen wings to melt, and he fell into the sea and drowned. Inconsolable Daedalus buried his son on a nearby island, naming it Ikaria.

Ikaria is a mountainous and green island, with an area of about 255 square kilometres, located 60 kilometres from the Turkish coast. It is yet another Mediterranean island that was, for a time, under the rule of the Knights of St John, later known as the Knights of Malta. In the mid-16th century, the island fell under Ottoman rule, but due to the stubbornness and poverty of the local population, the Turks never really imposed their way of life or rules on the people. The relatively peaceful life of the inhabitants of Ikaria changed during the Greek War of Independence, when Ikaria seceded from the faltering **Ottoman Empire** in 1827, hoping to join the newly established **Kingdom of Greece**. Unfortunately, the peace treaty did not foresee such a development, so Ikaria was returned to the Ottomans, under whose rule it remained for over 80 years.

At the beginning of July 1912, the population of Ikaria initiated a rebellion and quickly expelled the Turkish army from the island. With this courageous action, Ikaria became independent, and on 18 July, the Free State of Ikaria was proclaimed. The leader of the uprising, Dr Ioannis Malachias, was proclaimed the first and, as it turned out, only president. After the success of the **Balkan states** in the First Balkan War, on 4 November, 1912, Ikaria became part of the Greek state, officially confirmed by the Treaty of London in 1913.

During its brief existence, the Free State of Ikaria adopted a flag, an anthem, armed forces, and government, and even issued its own postage stamps. However, at the same time, it suffered from food shortages and feared the possibility of being forcibly annexed to the Italian islands of the Aegean Sea. Agios Kirykos was chosen as the capital. The island microstate had one military ship under its command, although it was primarily used for delivering food from the neighbouring larger islands of Samos and Chios. The small nearby archipelago of Fournoi was liberated from Turkish rule and also joined the Free State of Ikaria.

Despite the unification with **Greece**, many inhabitants of Ikaria were dissatisfied with the low level of investment in their island. After the Second World War, Ikaria was used as a place of exile for political opponents, primarily communists, which is why it was nicknamed the Red Rock. One of the most famous exiles was Mikis Theodorakis, the renowned Greek politician and composer, known for composing the music for the film *Zorba the Greek* and numerous other musical masterpieces.

ISLE OF MAN

Holding its own between Britain and Ireland

LOCATION: Irish Sea
PERIOD: since 1399
AREA: 572 sq km
POPULATION: 84,519

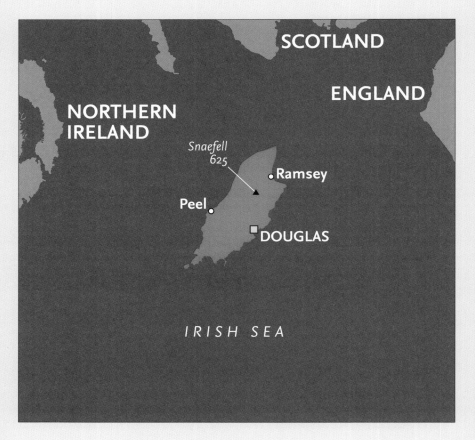

SCOTLAND

ENGLAND

NORTHERN
IRELAND

Snaefell
625

Ramsey

Peel

DOUGLAS

IRISH SEA

0   30 km

The **British Isles** (or 'these islands' as often referred to on Ireland) consist of two independent states – Ireland and the United Kingdom – and three territories under the rule of the British Crown, but with a high degree of autonomy and independence. The British Crown dependencies are the Channel Islands of **Jersey** and **Guernsey**, as well as the Isle of Man.

The Isle of Man is a self-governing island, situated in the middle of the Irish Sea, equidistant from the neighbouring islands of Ireland and Great Britain. The island is ruled by the monarch of the United Kingdom, who locally holds the title Lord of Mann. The British government is responsible for the isle's military defence and foreign policy, while all other matters fall under the jurisdiction of the government and parliament of the Isle of Man. The Tynwald, the parliament of the Isle of Man, reportedly established over 1,000 years ago, was the world's first parliament that granted women the right to vote, in the late 19th century, and was one of the first to lower the voting age to 16.

The relationship between the Isle of Man and the **UK** originated back in the mid-13th century when Norway ceded control of the Isle of Man to Scotland, which handed over the island to England in 1399. Since then, the 52-kilometre-long and 22-kilometre-wide island has been under the rule of the British crown. It has never been a part of England, Great Britain, or the European Union. The inhabitants of the island speak English and **Manx**, a Celtic language closely related to Irish and Scottish Gaelic, with the influence of the Old Norse language of Viking conquerors from the 9th century. The language was declared extinct in 1974, when the last native speaker died, but a relatively successful revival effort has resulted in around 2,000 people speaking or using the language again today.

The Isle of Man is home to the Manx cat, a unique breed of cat without a tail or with a very short one; the Manx Loaghtan, a breed of sheep with four or six powerful horns; and the Red-necked wallaby, an animal that many might mistake for a slightly small kangaroo. This marsupial, originating from southeastern Australia and Tasmania, found favourable living conditions on the Isle of Man when a pair escaped from Curraghs Wildlife Park in the 1960s and settled in the marshy area of Ballaugh Curraghs. It is estimated that there are around 600 free-roaming wallabies on the Isle of Man today.

Cinema and TV production bring significant revenue to the island, and tourism is becoming an increasingly important sector of the economy. The Isle of Man TT (Tourist Trophy) attracts a great deal of attention from visitors and has been held regularly since 1907. It is one of the most prestigious, and dangerous, motorcycle races in the world. Motorcyclists compete on closed public roads, totalling 60 kilometres in length. The race is demanding and fast – on certain sections, drivers reach speeds of more than 320 kilometres per hour, while the next moment, they have to navigate through small village streets with sharp bends.

Manx Loaghtan is a four-horned (rarely six-horned) sheep native to the Isle of Man. The name comes from the Manx expression 'lugh dhoan' which means 'brown like a mouse'.

The Parliament of the Principality of Liechtenstein in Vaduz. Above it, the palace of the Prince can be seen.

PRINCIPALITY OF
LIECHTENSTEIN

Tiny but Olympian

LOCATION: Alpine region of central Europe
PERIOD: since 1719
AREA: 160 sq km
POPULATION: 39,327

Lake Constance

Rhine

SWITZERLAND

AUSTRIA

Schaan

VADUZ

Balzers

A l p s

0   10 km

Approximately 25 kilometres from north to south, and 8 kilometres from east to west, Liechtenstein is one of the smallest countries in the world. Located in the Alps region, tucked between **Austria** and **Switzerland**, today it is also one of the richest countries. It was founded in the early 18th century, when the Austrian noble family Liechtenstein bought the Lordship of Schellenberg and the County of Vaduz. With the unification of these two feudal areas in 1719, the Principality of Liechtenstein was created as one of the members of the **Holy Roman Empire**, which was a powerful union of a huge number of miniature German states. The creation of this new principality enabled a member of the Liechtenstein family to become a member of the prestigious parliament of the Holy Roman Empire and to have closer relations with the emperors themselves. However, this was not incentive enough for them to move from their Liechtenstein castle just outside of Vienna – in fact, the first visit to the country by a member of the Liechtenstein family was a full 100 years after the principality was declared! The first prince to actually live in his Alpine estate was Franz Joseph II, who moved from Vienna to Liechtenstein in 1938, just a few days after the 'Anschluss' (annexation) of Austria into **Nazi Germany**.

Today, Liechtenstein is a constitutional monarchy, in which the prince still has extensive powers. Due to its small size, it has always maintained close ties with its neighbours – with Austria-Hungary before the First World War, and with Switzerland from 1923, with which it has been in a customs and trade union ever since. As a result, Liechtenstein uses the Swiss franc, and Switzerland is largely responsible for the foreign policy and defence of its micro-neighbour. Liechtenstein consists of 11 municipalities, grouped into two units – Unterland (lower land) and Oberland (upper land). What is unusual about the municipalities is that many of them consist of a large number of enclaves and exclaves located on the territories of neighbouring municipalities (the capital, Vaduz, has as many as six exclaves). Another particularity is the fact that each municipality has the right to call a referendum, in which residents can express their opinion on the possibility of secession from the **Alpine Principality**. So far, no municipality has ever used this option.

Liechtenstein is one of only two countries in the world (the other being Uzbekistan) that are double-landlocked countries, meaning that they are landlocked, as are all their neighbours.

Despite being the fourth smallest country in Europe and the sixth smallest in the world, Liechtenstein has a lot to offer: majestic mountains (the Principality is the only country located completely in the Alps), extremely charming villages, the beautiful River Rhine and an exceptionally high quality of life, all under the watchful eyes of one of Europe's oldest noble families. This microstate is also the owner of the largest number of Olympic medals per capita – the ten medals won so far amount to one medal per approximately 3,900 inhabitants.

PRINCIPALITY OF
LIPPE

The scene of an 82-year reign

LOCATION: North Rhine-Westphalia, Germany
PERIOD: 1789–1918
AREA: 1,215 sq km
POPULATION: 150,000

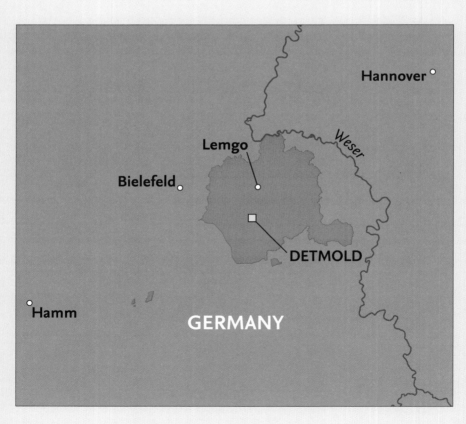

Hannover

Lemgo

Bielefeld

Weser

DETMOLD

Hamm

GERMANY

0 30 km

For hundreds of years, the territory of present-day **Germany** was divided among dozens of miniature states, connected in a loose alliance known as the Holy Roman Empire. There were occasional conflicts among these small states, and they often disregarded the authority of the Emperor.

One of these numerous small German states was the Principality of Lippe, located on the edge of the famous Teutoburg Forest, a possible site of the decisive battle from the 9th century when the Germans dealt the final blow to the Romans. The foundation for the formation of this small state was laid by Bernhard I, who received the piece of land from the Holy Roman Emperor in the early 12th century. From that moment, the history of this state and its ruling family began. The titles of the rulers changed over time, starting as Lord at Lippe, to Count in the 16th century, and Prince in 1789. Just a few years later, under pressure from Napoleon (of course, he gets involved in this story as well), the Holy Roman Empire ceased to exist, and a larger number of German states formed the Confederation of the Rhine, an ally of the **French Empire**. Lippe was among the members of the new confederation, headed by Princess Pauline as the regent of her underage son. This capable woman decided to abolish serfdom, wrote a relatively democratic constitution, and established numerous organisations for the social care of abandoned children and other vulnerable segments of the population. At the same time, she used all her ruling and political skills to ensure a high level of independence for her microstate, despite the tricky surroundings.

After the defeat of Napoleon and the Congress of Vienna in 1815, many borders in Europe were altered, and a significant number of states simply disappeared by being annexed by their neighbours. In Germany, states scrambled from one confederation to the next, and after the Confederation of the Rhine dissolved, Lippe maintained its independence by joining its replacement – the newly formed **German Confederation**, a union consisting of several dozen states. The small duchy managed to survive in the new conditions, and after the dissolution of the German Confederation in 1866, it joined the North German Confederation. When the unification of all German states was finally achieved, and the German Empire was formed, the Duchy of Lippe became one of the member states of this new European superpower.

The end of the First World War, and the proclamation of the German Republic, also meant the end of the monarchy in Lippe, and it transformed into the Free State of Lippe, a constituent element of the Weimar Republic. After the Second World War, Lippe joined the federal state of **North Rhine-Westphalia** but as a separate district, which has largely retained the borders of the extinguished Duchy to this day.

It is interesting that Bernard VII is usually considered the longest-reigning European monarch, after ruling Lippe for 82 whole years in the 15th and 16th centuries. One of his distant relatives is now on the throne of the Netherlands – King Willem-Alexander, who is a direct descendant of the House of Lippe through his mother's bloodline.

HOSPITALLER MALTA

All crusades lead to Malta

LOCATION: present-day Malta
PERIOD: 1530–1798
AREA: 316 sq km
POPULATION: 100,000

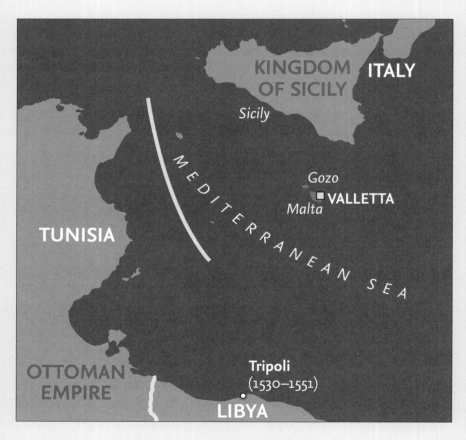

0   150 km

The Knights Hospitaller, a Catholic military order, began their journey in the Crusader **Kingdom of Jerusalem** in the 12th century, with the aim of helping sick pilgrims in the Holy Land. Later, they combined caring for the sick with crusading against the Muslims. When Jerusalem fell into the hands of the Muslims, they first fled to **Cyprus** and then to Rhodes, where they were based from the 14th to the 16th century. The power of the Ottomans was overwhelming, so in the first half of the 16th century, the Knights had to move again, this time to Malta, where they arrived in 1530.

The Knights received the islands of Malta and Gozo, as well as the city of Tripoli in present-day Libya, from Charles V, the Holy Roman Emperor and the King of Sicily. In exchange, the Knights had to abide by certain rules, one of which was to send one Maltese falcon to Sicily every year. The Ottomans soon conquered Tripoli, but their siege of Malta was unsuccessful. Shortly after this victory, the Knights decided to stay in Malta permanently, and began building Valletta, the new capital of their state known as Hospitaller Malta (around the same time, the port of Valletta was hit by one of the strongest tornadoes ever recorded, claiming more than 600 lives). Over the next 200 years, art and general progress flourished in Malta, with the construction of numerous new fortifications. The building of a 26-kilometre-long aqueduct enabled the regular supply of water to Valletta from 1615 until the early 20th century. On Malta, the Knights minted their currency called scudo.

In the middle of the 17th century, the Knights of Malta bought four **Caribbean islands** (St Christopher, St-Martin, St-Barthélemy, and St Croix), making it the smallest European colonial power in the Americas at that time. After 14 years, the Knights sold their colonial rights to France, but even today, the famous Maltese cross is featured on the coat of arms of St-Barthélemy. This cross has been the official symbol of the Hospitaller Knights since the early 12th century and is recognisable by its eight points, symbolising the eight obligations (truth, faith, mercy, repentance, humility, justice, sincerity, and endurance) of each knight.

Hospitaller Malta was a vassal state of the **Kingdom of Sicily** until 1753 when the Order of Knights declared complete independence. However, the end of the 18th century brought a severe blow to the Order: all their possessions in France were confiscated, which drained their financial resources. In 1798, Napoleon occupied the state of the Knights of Malta, and two years later, Britain took over Malta from the French. Although there was an agreement for the British to return Malta to the Order, this never happened, and Malta remained a British colony until gaining independence in 1964. In the meantime, the Knights once again left their stronghold, establishing new headquarters in their two villas in Rome, which remain extraterritorial properties of the Sovereign Military Order of Malta to this day.

REPUBLIC OF
MALTA

The land of honey

LOCATION: Central Mediterranean
PERIOD: since 1964
AREA: 316 sq km
POPULATION: 533,286

Victoria

Gozo

Comino

MEDITERRANEAN SEA

Mosta

VALLETTA

Mdina

Malta

▲ 253

0   10 km

The Mediterranean Sea has 5,000–10,000 islands, depending on how an island is defined. Out of this vast number, only **Cyprus** and Malta are independent island countries.

The Republic of Malta is situated in the central part of the Mediterranean. Although it is one of the smallest countries in the world in terms of its area, it is one of the most densely populated. It is a country with an extremely rich history, where one can see ancient megalithic monuments built over 5,500 years ago, as well as endless networks of underground tunnels and catacombs from the same period. Additionally, throughout Malta, one can see 'cart tracks', traces of wooden-wheeled carts which carved grooves into the limestone several thousand years ago. At least this is one of the presumptions regarding the origin of these mysterious channels...

Malta is an archipelago consisting of three larger inhabited islands (Malta, Gozo and Comino) and several smaller uninhabited islands and rocks, located on the African tectonic plate. This Mediterranean microstate is subject to frequent droughts, partly caused by the fact that there are no permanent rivers or lakes on any of the archipelago's islands, although there are several small springs and streams. On the other hand, its warm climate and approximately 300 sunny days per year have made Malta a popular tourist destination.

The strategic position of Malta made it a desirable land for regional and global powers, leading to numerous changes in rulers throughout history. As explored in the previous pages, Hospitaller Malta was ruled by the Knights Hospitaller, or the Knights of Malta, who were briefly replaced by the French in the early 19th century. From 1800 until 1964, Malta was under British rule. The independent State of Malta recognised Queen Elizabeth II as the Queen of Malta until 1974 when the Republic of Malta was declared. Exactly 30 years later, Malta became a member of the European Union. Today, Malta is a highly urbanised country, often viewed as a single urban region and a city-state.

The Maltese language is one of the two official languages in Malta (the other being English). Maltese originates from the Sicilian Arabic language spoken in **Sicily** during Islamic rule from the 9th to the 11th century. Today, it is the only Semitic language written in the Latin alphabet and the only Semitic language that is official within the EU. Italian, Sicilian, and English have had a significant influence on the formation of the modern Maltese language.

A subspecies of bee that only lives in Malta is known for producing unusually large amounts of honey. Perhaps this is the reason why the **Ancient Greeks** named the island *Melite*, meaning '(island) of honey', which is the etymology of the present-day name of Malta, a small, sweet island surrounded by a vast, salty sea.

MEMEL TERRITORY

An ice-free port of the Baltic Sea

LOCATION: Baltic Coast, present-day Lithuania
PERIOD: 1919–1923
AREA: 2,660 sq km
POPULATION: 140,000

The 1919 Treaty of Versailles marked the formal end of the First World War, clearly defining the conditions of peace between the Allies and the Central Powers. An important element of the treaty was the creation of new borders, leading to the disappearance of some states (Austria-Hungary) and the formation of new ones (Poland, Yugoslavia), as well as the partial redrawing of the borders of defeated Germany. Certain German territories were granted to neighbouring countries (France, Belgium, Denmark, Poland), with the simultaneous establishment of territories under the control of the Allies or the League of Nations. One such area was the so-called Memel Territory or **Klaipėda Region**.

The northernmost part of the German province of **East Prussia** sat around the large port of Memel (Lithuanian: Klaipėda), situated between the Neman River, the Baltic Sea, and the border of **Lithuania** at that time. It was separated from Germany by the Treaty of Versailles and placed under the administration of the Entente's Council of Ambassadors. It was planned that this narrow strip of land, approximately 140 kilometres in length and 20 kilometres in width, would function for some time as an autonomous condominium (an area under the joint administration of the Allies). After this period, a referendum would be held, allowing the citizens to vote on whether or not they wanted to be under the auspices of **Germany**. Poland and France, whose military garrison was responsible for maintaining order in the Memel area, were in favour of the entire Memelland (German name) or Klaipėdos kraštas (Lithuanian name) to belong to Lithuania, but with Lithuania itself to be forced to join Poland. As expected, Lithuania and Germany were opposed to such a solution, while three-quarters of the local population of Memel supported the idea of creating the Free State of Memel, similar to the **Free City of Danzig**, which was formed from the easternmost part of the German province of West Prussia.

When the authorities of Lithuania realised that there was growing desire among the great powers to create a Free State, they decided to act quickly. With covert support from the Lithuanian government, demonstrations and protests were organised throughout Memel Territory. The protesters overthrew the local pro-German government (Directorate), and on 13 January 1923, a new Directorate was elected, this time pro-Lithuanian. One of the first tasks of the new government was to submit a request for annexation to Lithuania, which the Lithuanian parliament approved on 24 January. Consequently, the Republic of Lithuania incorporated the Klaipėda Region as an autonomous area, with its own parliament (in all elections until the Second World War, pro-German parties consistently won a convincing majority), two official languages (Lithuanian and German), separate citizenship, and customs and tax regulations. Lithuania had gained a strategically important ice-free port in the city of Memel/Klaipėda. After the Second World War, Memel/Klaipėda remained part of (Soviet) Lithuania, while the rest of East Prussia, south of the Neman River, was divided between Poland and the Soviet Union, forming the exclave Kaliningrad Oblast.

PRINCIPALITY OF
MONACO

City of luxury, history and grace

LOCATION: French Riviera
PERIOD: since 1297
AREA: 2 sq km
POPULATION: 36,469

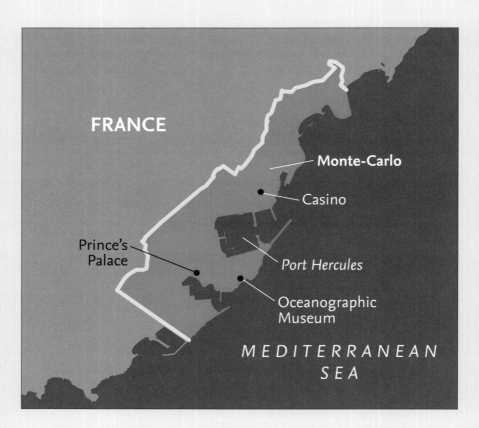

FRANCE

Monte-Carlo

Casino

Prince's
Palace

Port Hercules

Oceanographic
Museum

*MEDITERRANEAN
SEA*

0   1 km

The French Riviera, or **Côte d'Azur** in French, represents the easternmost part of the French Mediterranean coast, extending all the way to the border with **Italy**. This region is a glamorous destination, attracting numerous tourists with its charm, natural beauty, luxurious style, and diverse cultural heritage. Among the most famous communes along the coast are Menton and St-Tropez and the cities Nice, Cannes, and Monaco. The latter is, in fact, a sovereign city-state and the epicentre of the global jet-set lifestyle.

Monaco is a principality whose history began in 1297 when Francesco Grimaldi seized the fortress and established the rule of the Grimaldi dynasty. In 1419, the Grimaldi family purchased Monaco from the Crown of Aragon, becoming the formal rulers of the tiny principality. The Grimaldis continue to rule Monaco to this day, and the inheritance often passes down the female line, with a prince adopting his wife's Grimaldi surname. This was the case with the grandfather of Albert II, the current Prince of Monaco.

The Principality is situated on hilly terrain, so stepped buildings are often constructed to make the most of the limited land available. Monaco has been expanding since 1880 when land reclamation projects began, creating valuable hectares of new land. The latest project was completed in 2020, adding six hectares for future construction of theatres, museums, and other buildings. Despite land reclamation, Monaco remains the second-smallest sovereign state in the world by land area, just behind the Vatican, while having the highest population density of any nation on the entire planet. It is surrounded on three sides by France and is only about ten kilometres away from the Italian border. Interestingly, of the 36,469 residents, only 22% are native **Monégasques**, with the largest community being French, making up nearly 25%. Therefore, it is not surprising that French is the official language of the Principality, and the national language, Monégasque, is scarcely used outside of schools, where it was introduced as a mandatory subject in 1976.

A lot of well-known personalities have found their (permanent or temporary) home in Monaco. Although the Principality was known before, the marriage in 1956 of Prince Rainier III and the famous Hollywood film star Grace Kelly drew the attention of the world media to this microstate, with over 30 million viewers watching the wedding live on television. Among those who have had, or currently have, their residence in Monaco are actor Sir Roger Moore, Formula 1 driver Sir Lewis Hamilton, singer Dame Shirley Bassey, and one of the greatest tennis players of all time, Novak Djoković.

Monaco takes up barely 2 square kilometres, yet there has been space to place a large number of famous buildings in the only Mediterranean principality, including the magnificent Prince's Palace, the Monte-Carlo Casino, and the renowned Oceanographic Museum. Monaco also excels in sports, with the world-famous Monaco Grand Prix, and the very successful football team AS Monaco FC, adding to its prestige.

NEUTRAL
MORESNET

Place of many friendships

LOCATION: present-day eastern Belgium
PERIOD: 1816–1920
AREA: 3.5 sq km
POPULATION: C. 3,000

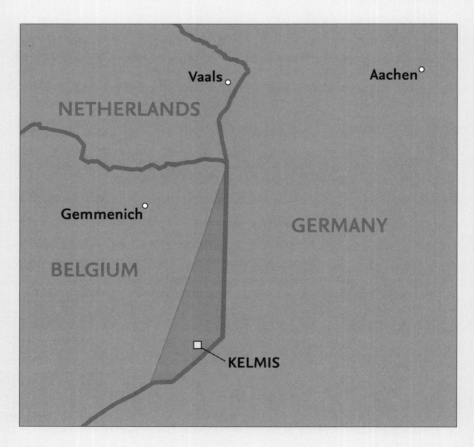

0   3 km

The defeat of Napoleon Bonaparte in 1815 led to the Congress of Vienna, where the main task was the redrawing of new borders after the collapse of the **French Empire**. A great number of disagreements over the new borders were resolved in various ways, often by the formation of small semi-independent city-states. One such case involved Vieille Montagne, at that time the largest zinc mine in Europe, which both the Netherlands and Prussia wanted to claim. Unable to agree on who should own the mine, they reached a compromise: the mine and the town next to it would become the neutral territory of Moresnet, a condominium of both the Netherlands and Prussia.

Neutral Moresnet had a triangular shape, 5 kilometres in length and 1.5 kilometres at its widest. The territory was governed by two royal commissioners from the neighbouring kingdoms, who jointly appointed the mayor. An advisory municipal council was formed in 1859, and slightly greater self-administration was granted to Moresnet. All laws in this microstate were based on the Civil Code of the French, a set of legal norms enacted during Napoleon's time as the First Consul of the French Republic.

The main economic driving force of Moresnet was the mining company, serving as the largest employer and owning almost all the residences, banks, and shops. Significant benefits to the inhabitants were the low taxes, the absence of import tariffs, and generally lower prices compared to those in the **Netherlands** and **Prussia**.

Despite multiple geopolitical changes, Moresnet remained a condominium – first of the Netherlands and Prussia, then of Belgium and Prussia (after Belgium gained its independence from the Netherlands in 1830), and finally of **Belgium** and **Germany**, when Prussia initiated the formation of the German Empire in 1871. After Belgium separated from the Netherlands, the former tripoint (a triple border point) of the Netherlands, Prussia, and Moresnet became a quadripoint (a quadruple border point) involving the Netherlands, Belgium, Prussia, and Moresnet. Quadripoints are very rare, and there are none in the world today. However, even this one was not a true quadripoint, as Moresnet was not a sovereign state.

The problems for Moresnet began when the zinc mine was exhausted in 1885. At the beginning of the 20th century, Moresnet attempted to generate income by opening a casino, which Germany quickly terminated, as well as by opening several gin distilleries.

Moresnet has a special place in the **Esperanto** community because, in 1908, there was a proposal for this area to become the first country where Esperanto was spoken, with the suggestion to change the name of the microstate to Amikejo ('place of friendship').

Unfortunately, all those ideas were forgotten with the outbreak of the First World War and the German occupation of Moresnet. The peace treaty of 1919, known as the Treaty of Versailles, heralded the end of Neutral Moresnet, and the following year it was assigned to Belgium, along with several neighbouring German towns. Today, this area constitutes the municipality of Kelmis, part of the German-speaking community of Belgium, and many border markers of Moresnet are still clearly standing, testifying to the existence of the former 'place of friendship'.

MOUNT ATHOS

Where Byzantine time still stands

LOCATION: Aegean Sea, Greece
PERIOD: since 972 CE
AREA: 336 sq km
POPULATION: C. 2,000

0   30 km

Centuries after the fall of the (Eastern) Roman Empire, known as the **Byzantium Empire**, a small peninsula in **Greece** still bases its everyday life on the Byzantine and Christian traditions of past times. This peninsula is Mount Athos, known as the 'third finger' part of the larger Chalkidiki peninsula, a significant tourist centre in northern Greece. Mount Athos (in Greek, Oros Athos), extending along the entire length of the peninsula like a spine, has its highest peak at 2,033 metres. The peninsula is about 50 kilometres long and 7 to 12 kilometres wide, and is crisscrossed with a network of footpaths, many of which were well-trodden back in the Byzantine era.

Although it formally belongs to Greece, almost the entire peninsula constitutes the semi-autonomous Monastic Community of Mount Athos (Agion Oros), home to around 2,000 Orthodox monks. They live, work, and pray in 20 monasteries and numerous smaller establishments scattered on the magnificent cliffs and small valleys throughout the peninsula. Due to the exceptional cultural treasures held by the monasteries – including rare books, ancient documents, and priceless artworks – the entire monastic state has been listed as a **UNESCO World Heritage Site**.

The peninsula became self-governing in 972 CE, when the first charter of the monastic community was signed by Byzantine Emperor John I Tzimiskes. Since then, the community has endured numerous hardships, including the brutal rule of the Crusaders and raids of the peninsula by the Catalan mercenaries in the 14th century, which led to the prohibition of access to the Holy Mountain for people of Catalan origin until the early years of the 21st century. Occasional periods of prosperity, such as during the exceptionally generous rule of the Serbian Emperor Stefan Dušan, were followed by gloomy times such as that under Ottoman rule, although the sultans did preserve at least some elements of autonomy for the Orthodox peninsula. A similar situation occurred during the Second World War when Mount Athos, at the request of the monks, was under the direct protection of Adolf Hitler.

The administration of the peninsula is held by a collective body comprising all 20 monasteries, with its headquarters located in the main settlement of Karyes, which is also home to the Civil Administrator, a representative of the Greek Ministry of Foreign Affairs. The supreme church authority belongs to the Ecumenical Patriarch of Constantinople, with the majority of monks being ethnically Greek, and a significant number of Russians, Serbs, Romanians, Bulgarians, and others.

There are two interesting facts that distinguish Mount Athos from all other states or autonomous territories. The first is that only males are allowed to stay there. Due to the strict celibacy of the monks, women are entirely prohibited from accessing all monasteries and the entire territory of the monastic republic – even just for short visits – despite the fact that it is formally a part of Greece and the **European Union**. The second curiosity concerns the expression of time: 'Byzantine time' was used during the Byzantine Empire and is still followed on Mount Athos today, whereby the first hour of the day begins at dusk, rather than at midnight.

REPUBLIC OF
MULHOUSE

Run of the mill, it is not

LOCATION: Eastern France
PERIOD: 1308–1798
AREA: 29 sq km
POPULATION: c. 8,000

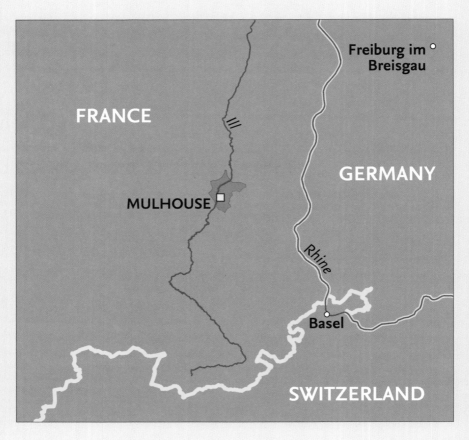

Situated close to the France–Switzerland–Germany tripoint, the picturesque city of Mulhouse has a unique history.

Mulhouse is said to have been founded in the early 9th century around a watermill, hence its name in German and the local Alsatian German dialect, *Mülhausen* or *Mìlhüsa* ('Mill House'). The city's coat of arms and flag have portrayed a water mill for over 1,000 years. Like the rest of the Alsace region, Mulhouse was part of the **Holy Roman Empire**. After the inhabitants of the city managed to free themselves from the direct rule of the prince-bishop of Strasbourg at the end of the 13th century, Mulhouse became a free imperial city in 1308 and a de facto independent city-republic 40 years later. Between 1354 and 1515, along with nine other free imperial cities of **Alsace**, it formed a defensive alliance known as the *Décapole*, in French, or the *Zehnstädtebund* in German, meaning 'ten cities'.

The broad autonomy and rapid development of the city led to jealous glances from the surrounding nobility, especially the powerful Habsburg family. In order to protect itself, Mulhouse severed ties with Alsace, and in 1515 became an associate member of the so-called Old Swiss Confederation (although first agreements with individual cantons had already been signed as early as 1466). In actuality this meant breaking away from the Holy Roman Empire, which proved to be a wise move by the mid-17th century. At that time, the Peace of Westphalia was signed, allowing France to occupy the entire Alsace region... except Mulhouse, which was then an autonomous part of **Switzerland**.

Mulhouse, officially known as Stadtrepublik Mülhausen, remained a free republic, a Swiss Calvinist enclave in the predominantly Lutheran Alsace, in **France**. It was a conservative city with strict religious rules, such as the prohibition of leaving the city during church services or the obligation to wear modest, simple clothing. The only permitted religion was Christianity of the Calvinist type.

The progress of industrialisation led to the easing of religious rules. Soon, one after another, modern textile factories were opened, their number reaching more than 15 by the end of the 18th century. Chemical and machine industries soon followed the textile industry, thanks to which Mulhouse later become known as the 'French Manchester', after Britain's hub of industrialisation.

However, the economic crisis that struck France at the end of the 18th century led to strong pressure on the small Republic, where unemployment and food prices began to rise rapidly. Switzerland showed no desire to help its associate member, and the authorities of Mulhouse made a difficult decision in 1798: they abandoned the alliance with Switzerland and decided to merge the Republic of Mulhouse into France. With this agreement, France finally gained control over the entire Alsace region after 150 years, and the former Fräija Repüblik Mìlhüsa is now a city with more than 100,000 inhabitants within the European Collectivity of Alsace.

REPUBLIC OF **NOLI**

A state outlived by its beauty

LOCATION: Liguria, Italy
PERIOD: 1192–1797
AREA: 4 sq km
POPULATION: C. 1,500

Alessandria

Cuneo

I T A L Y

Genova
Genoa

Savona

Gulf of Genoa

Savona

NOLI

LIGURIAN
SEA

0   20 km

When the representatives of the small town of Noli purchased a castle and other noble rights from Henry VI, Emperor of the Holy Roman Empire, in 1192, they couldn't have known they initiated a story that would last for more than six centuries. By signing the imperial decree in the church in Noli, the foundation of a new micro-republic was laid on the coast of the Ligurian Sea, not far from Genoa.

The Republic of Noli consisted of a single city, two nearby villages, and a small island, not far from the approximately 4-kilometre-long coastline. It was an oligarchic republic, meaning that the state was ruled by several families. The state was governed by the Podestà (a title that usually denoted the mayor of the city-state), the Council of Consuls and the Council of Heads of Houses. Despite its small size, the Republic had a relatively strong economy, based on high-quality shipbuilding, glass production, fishing, olive growing, and trade with the neighbouring **Republic of Genoa**, a regional power. Interestingly, Noli never minted its own currency; instead, Genoese currency was used throughout its existence.

The neighbours of Noli, the Marquisate of Finale and the County of Savona, were often aggressive towards this microstate. This forced Noli to form a kind of confederation with Genoa in 1202, which thus became the protector of the small Republic. This defensive alliance lasted until 1797.

The Repubbrica de Nöi was the official name of this small maritime state in the Ligurian language. The majority of the population spoke Ligurian, a Gallo-Romance language, today widespread in the Liguria region – roughly between Genoa and **Monaco** – as well as in **Gibraltar** and several settlements on the islands of Sardinia and Corsica. Noli created its flag (red with a white cross) as a contrast to the flag of its major protector, the Republic of Genoa (white with a red cross). The flag of the Republic of Noli still flies on the palace, which was the seat of the Podestà and the government. The fact that in 1239, Pope Gregory IX declared Noli an independent diocese of the Catholic Church proves the importance this small Republic once had.

There are numerous factors that led to the decline of the influence and wealth of Noli. As ships grew larger, so did the nearby ports, something Noli could not keep up with. At the same time, frequent disputes among the ruling families arose and several deadly epidemics of infectious diseases became a problem for the city.

Who knows how long this story would have lasted if Napoleon Bonaparte had not intervened again, as he began his campaign against Italy in 1797. The Republic of Noli managed to maintain its independence for three months longer than its ally and protector, Genoa. The entire region of present-day **Liguria** was incorporated into the French puppet state, the Ligurian Republic, which was directly annexed to the First French Empire a few years later. After its collapse, it became part of the Kingdom of Sardinia, and in 1861, the Kingdom of **Italy**. Today, Noli is a member of the association *I Borghi più belli d'Italia* ('The most beautiful villages of Italy'), which is no small matter for the former small Republic.

REPUBLIC OF
PAULAVA

A utopic state ahead of its time

LOCATION: Lithuania
PERIOD: 1769–1795
AREA: 30 sq km
POPULATION: c. 800

Paweł Ksawery Brzostowski was a Polish noble and Catholic priest, who lived from 1739 to 1827. He held various important ecclesiastical and secular positions in the Polish-Lithuanian Commonwealth, the union of the Kingdom of **Poland** and the Grand Duchy of **Lithuania**. However, for a little over a quarter of a century, he was the president of a small – yet exceptionally democratic and progressive, for its time – micro-republic.

At around the age of 30, Brzostowski purchased Merkinė Manor, a derelict estate covering approximately 3,000 hectares, not far from Vilnius, the present-day capital of Lithuania. Immediately after the purchase, he declared his estate an independent state named the Republic of Paulava, after his own name (Lithuanian: Paulavos respublika; Polish: Rzeczpospolita Pawłowska). However, what followed was almost unthinkable for that time period: he freed his serfs from the obligation of forced labour on the estate; he divided the land among the already liberated peasants, who rented it from him, the owner; and he allowed peasants to engage in trade and various crafts. He continued in this vein by building schools (including for women, which was hard to imagine at that time); translating books for the peasants; and he invested a great deal in healthcare. He introduced agriculture as a mandatory subject in schools, and encouraged peasants to engage in more profitable agricultural production, such as growing fruit. The result was a significant increase in yields on estates throughout the small republic.

At the very beginning of its existence, Paulava adopted a liberal constitution, which established the rights and obligations of all citizens. The constitution also defined the existence of a local parliament, courts, and a small army of about a hundred people – all composed of peasants from Paulava. The parliament elected Brzostowski as its lifelong president. Despite being small in both size and population, the Republic of Paulava was soon recognised as an autonomous state by Stanisław August Poniatowski, the King of Poland and Grand Duke of Lithuania, as well as by the Great Sejm, the parliament of the **Polish-Lithuanian Commonwealth**. Some historians go so far as to claim that Paulava can be seen as the third (almost) equal member of this powerful union.

Paulava shared the unfortunate fate of its larger neighbours, Poland and Lithuania. All three states ceased to exist in 1795, after Russia, Prussia, and Austria executed the so-called Third Partition of Poland, which led to the end of Poland and Lithuania as independent states until 1918. President Brzostowski traded his microstate for an estate in Saxony, and the rights of his free citizens were partially respected until his death in 1827.

Today, all that remains of this small utopian state are the ruins of the presidential palace, designed in neoclassical style in 1770. This beautiful building survived two world wars, but according to some sources, it was almost completely destroyed in a (possibly deliberate) fire during the Soviet era. Today, the manor is a tourist attraction, the last remnants of a libertarian and democratic microstate far ahead of its time.

REPUBLIC OF
POLJICA

A state of elected dukes

LOCATION: Croatian coastal region
PERIOD: 1200s–1807
AREA: 250 sq km
POPULATION: C. 10,000

CROATIA

Cetina

Split

ADRIATIC
SEA

Omiš

Brač

0   10 km

The Middle Ages brought frequent wars and changes of power throughout Europe and the world, and people's lives were disrupted often by unstable governance. In the 13th century, such was the situation in Dalmatia, where the rule of the Hungarian kingdom, the **Republic of Venice**, Bosnian rulers, and later powerful Ottoman sultans, often alternated. This encouraged the local nobility and inhabitants from the area between Split and Omiš to gradually establish an autonomous region, with many elements of sovereignty and a significant salt production. This territory became known as Poljica. One assumption is that this name derives from the Slavic word *polje* (field), which today denotes a large flat plain found in karstic geological regions.

The Duchy of Poljica, or today more commonly, the Republic of Poljica, was a peasant autonomous community, whose population lived in several scattered villages. Each village was headed by a duke, with the entire republic ruled by a grand duke. Although the dukes were always of noble birth, they were elected to the position by all inhabitants of Poljica.

The political system of this microstate was based on the Poljica Statute, a unique document that regulated almost all aspects of functioning of the small republic. The oldest preserved version of the Statute dates back to 1440, although it is known that there was also an older version. This document was written in a special form of Cyrillic script, known as Poljica script. Initially, the Statute had about 20 articles, but over time, articles concerning trade, livestock farming, inheritance, and public roads were added, along with clear indications of strict penalties for all violations; emphasising every person's right to life, as well as the need for everyone to live in brotherhood and unity. Every change of suzerain (the state that had supreme authority over the autonomous Republic of Poljica) was an occasion to add new articles to this 'constitution'.

Although small in size and population, Poljica managed to preserve its semi-independence for about six centuries, despite frequent attacks from its neighbours. The area was difficult to access, because of surrounding rugged mountains that largely served as the natural defence system of the entire region. Two great victories are well known, in 1530 and 1686, against military attacks of the **Ottoman Empire**. According to a local legend, in 1530, a young woman named Mila Gojsalić succeeded in blowing up an Ottoman army munitions stockpile, killing the commander and a large number of Turkish soldiers, said to be up to 10,000 men. A renowned Croatian and Yugoslav sculptor created a sculpture of Mila Gojsalić, which still stands today on the hill above Omiš, guarding Poljica.

The end of the Republic of Poljica came in 1807 when its inhabitants gave aid to the Russians and Montenegrins during the battles against **France**. Napoleon was not pleased with this at all, so French troops conquered Poljica, brutally destroyed all villages and massacred a large number of inhabitants. The definitive end of the small, and at that time democratic, state occurred after Napoleon's fall when Poljica was simply annexed to the **Austrian Empire**.

Today, the former republic is divided across several Croatian municipalities, its glorious story consigned to history.

PONTECORVO

From city-state, to principality, to republic

LOCATION: present-day Italy

PERIOD: 1806–1815 (Principality)
1820–1821 (Republic)

AREA: 88 sq km

POPULATION: C. 3,000

ITALY

PONTECORVO

LIGURIAN
SEA

Naples

Salerno

0   50 km

Here is yet another (short-lived) mini-state made possible by Napoleon Bonaparte.

The town of Pontecorvo is located two-thirds of the way between Rome and Naples. In the mid-15th century, the city authorities decided to leave the **Kingdom of Naples**, which at that time encompassed the southern half of the Apennine Peninsula and the island of Sicily. They placed their city, as an enclave, under the authority of the Papal States, which lasted until the 19th century (a similar situation occurred with Benevento, another enclave of the Papal State within the territory of the Kingdom of Naples).

Pontecorvo was conquered by Napoleon's French troops at the beginning of the 19th century. When Napoleon declared himself King of Italy in 1805, he decided to reward one of his marshals for their successes in the Battle of Austerlitz, so he gave him Pontecorvo as a gift. The enclave thus became the formally independent Principality of Pontecorvo in 1806, and Marshal Jean Baptiste Bernadotte became the Sovereign Prince of Pontecorvo. Despite the name of the state and the title of its ruler, Pontecorvo functioned as one of the numerous puppet states of Napoleon's France.

Two interesting facts are associated with Marshal Bernadotte. The first is that he allegedly never set foot in his mini-state, probably because he was too busy commanding his troops and because of his consistently turbulent relationship with the French Emperor. The second is that this committed republican, only four years after receiving the title of Prince of Pontecorvo, by an unusual turn of events, was chosen as the heir-presumptive of Sweden and the supreme commander of the Swedish Armed Forces. When the previous crown prince suddenly died, the Swedish parliament decided to offer the crown to someone from Napoleon's family or closest circle. Bernadotte accepted the offer, and in 1818, he was crowned King of **Sweden** and **Norway** as Charles XIV John and Charles III John. During the final battles of the European allies against Napoleon, the Swedish ruler supported the allies in the battles against his former Emperor. Today's Swedish royal dynasty directly descends from the French Marshal and Prince of Pontecorvo, and the state coat of arms of the Kingdom of Sweden still features the curved bridge from the former duchy (the name Pontecorvo derives from the Latin term *pons curvus*, meaning 'curved bridge').

The fall of Napoleon's empire led to the downfall of numerous French puppet states across Europe. Such was the fate of Pontecorvo, which in 1815 was ceded back to the Papal States. However, only five years later, an anti-papal rebellion broke out in the enclave, resulting in the expulsion of the papal governor and the declaration of the free Republic of Pontecorvo. A provisional government was formed and immediately requested the Kingdom of Naples to accept it under its auspices. Unfortunately, Naples ignored this request, and the rebel republic soon succumbed to the pro-papal army, which occupied Pontecorvo in March 1821. Forty years later, all of these small states on the Apennine Peninsula disappeared, and a new powerful **Kingdom of Italy** emerged on the world stage.

REPUBLIC OF
RAGUSA

*Prosperous on and
off screen*

LOCATION: Southern Croatia
PERIOD: 1358–1808
AREA: 1,100 sq km
POPULATION: C. 90,000

The decision by HBO to use the southernmost Croatian city of **Dubrovnik** as the location for King's Landing, the capital of Westeros, in the television series *Game of Thrones*, was quite justified. The majestic ancient walls, magnificent buildings, and beauty of the city seem as though they were created for the capital of a mighty kingdom. Yet in real life, Dubrovnik was actually the capital of a microstate for hundreds of years – the Republic of Ragusa.

The Republic of Ragusa was a small but quite wealthy and influential maritime aristocratic republic in the vicinity of the city of Dubrovnik (known as Ragusa in Italian). It is assumed that the city was founded in the early 7th century, initially as two separate settlements, one Roman and the other Slavic. Over time, these two settlements merged, creating a unique city with the official Latin name Ragusa and the unofficial Slavic name Dubrovnik, from the Slavic word dubrava, meaning 'an oak grove' (the Slavic name became official only in 1918). In the first centuries of its existence, the city was ruled by **Byzantium, Venice**, and the Normans, and its territory expanded through acquisition and purchase of surrounding land. Ragusa, a city within the **Venetian Republic**, experienced its greatest expansion in the first half of the 14th century through the purchase of the large peninsula of Pelješac from the Serbian Emperor Stefan Dušan.

In 1358, Venice and Hungary signed the Treaty of Zadar, by which Venice renounced all its possessions in Dalmatia. Ragusa thus gained de facto independence, although it recognised the supreme authority of the Hungarian King Louis I. The small republic made good use of this – Hungary was not a naval power, so it allowed the vigorous development of the merchant fleet of its new vassal state. This beneficial situation continued even after the **Ottoman Empire** occupied large parts of the Western Balkans, when Ragusa accepted the Turkish sultan as its new suzerain. The favourable treaty that the Republic signed with the Ottomans enabled further development of trade and maritime affairs throughout Europe and the Mediterranean, even with countries with which the Ottoman Empire was at war.

In addition to trade, culture and science also flourished in Ragusa. Among its most famous poets was certainly Ivan Gundulić (Italian: Gianfrancesco Gondola), while Ruđer Bošković (Italian: Ruggero Giuseppe Boscovich) was one of the most significant astronomers and mathematicians in the world – he was the first to claim that there is no atmosphere around the Moon.

Napoleon once again brought about the end of a microstate: French troops occupied the neutral Republic of Ragusa in 1806, and in 1815, at the Congress of Vienna, this area was simply assigned to the Austrian Empire, where it remained until 1918.

By many standards, the Republic of Ragusa was a country ahead of its time. In 1416, it became the first European state to officially abolish enslavement, centuries before Britain and the United States. In the late 15th century, the Trsteno Arboretum was founded near the city of Ragusa, making it one of the oldest in Europe. The arboretum played a significant part in *Game of Thrones*, representing the gardens of the royal capital.

Trsteno Arboretum is located some twenty kilometres northwest of Dubrovnik. The oldest botanical garden in Croatia, it was founded by the Gučetić/Gozze aristocratic family from Raguza (Dubrovnik) at the end of the 15th century.

St-Malo Castle, also known as the castle of Duchess Anne of Brittany, was built in the 15th century to protect the city of St-Malo. The flags of the city, Brittany, France and the European Union are displayed on the walls of the fortress.

REPUBLIC OF
ST-MALO

*Not French, not Breton,
but Malouin*

LOCATION: Brittany, France
PERIOD: 1590–1594
AREA: under 10 sq km
POPULATION: C. 10,000

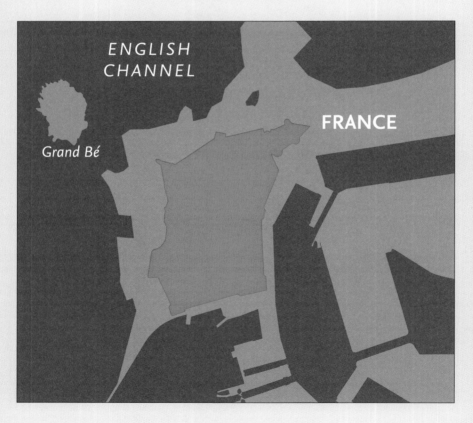

ENGLISH
CHANNEL

FRANCE

Grand Bé

0   0.5 km

In France, the second half of the 16th century was marked by several bloody wars between the Catholics and the Protestants, spanning over 35 years and resulting in the deaths of between two and four million people. Upon the death of King Henry III in 1589, another Henry III, a Protestant ruler of the Basque **Kingdom of Navarre**, succeeded him to the throne. After taking the French crown, the new King adopted the name Henry IV, but his rule was not acknowledged by many Catholic regions of France. One of these regions was the city of St-Malo, located on the northern coast of the historical region of Brittany, opposite the island of Jersey in the **English Channel**.

During the Wars of Religion, the inhabitants of St-Malo elected a council in 1585, whose main task was to protect the city from the dreadful consequences of the civil wars. The choice of a new Protestant king was not welcomed by the inhabitants of the predominantly Catholic city. When the King set out for St-Malo in early March 1590, a group of Malouins, as the inhabitants of the city were generally called, attacked the governor's castle. The governor and his associates were killed, sending a strong message to the King that he was not welcome.

The Council of St-Malo immediately took control of the city and castle, promising they would return the Republic to the protection of the French Kingdom when a Catholic king ascended the throne. The Independent Republic of St-Malo was declared with the motto 'Not French, not Breton, but Malouin'. The Council had control over all aspects of state sovereignty: foreign policy, finances, defence, and trade. Although they were opponents of the Protestant King of France, the Malouins continued free trade with **England**, the **Netherlands**, and cities in northern **Germany**.

The small republic led a wise foreign policy and simultaneously strengthened its military and merchant fleet, which sailed as far as the coasts of present-day **Brazil** and **Canada**. Such a strong fleet enabled fishing and trade with numerous countries, increasing the wealth throughout the city, whose warehouses were filled with a wide variety of goods.

However, in 1593, King Henry IV made a wise political move: he converted to Catholicism, knowing that this was the only way he could win over the predominantly Catholic population of France. When he was formally crowned King of France in 1594, the Council of St-Malo realised that there was no longer any justification for the existence of this microstate. The return of the Republic of St-Malo to the French crown was accelerated by Henry IV's promise of a general amnesty, and permission that all privileges, acquired from the time of brief independence, would remain in the hands of the Malouins.

Although its independence was brief, in the mid-18th century, St-Malo lent its name to islands more than 12,000 kilometres away. The Spanish name for the **Falkland Islands**, Islas Malvinas, is derived from the French name Îles Malouines. This name for the archipelago in the South Atlantic was given by the French explorer Louis-Antoine de Bougainville, whose ships set sail from a port that was 'not French, not Breton, but Malouin'.

PRINCIPALITY OF **SAMOS**

*The semi-independent
state of princes, Pythagoras
and Hera*

LOCATION: Aegean Sea, Greece
PERIOD: 1834–1912
AREA: 477 sq km
POPULATION: c. 55,000

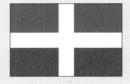

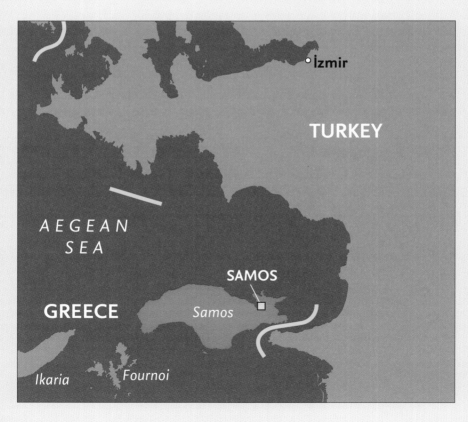

The Greek uprising against the ruling Ottoman Empire in 1821 led to the establishment of the independent Kingdom of Greece, initially encompassing the southern parts of present-day **Greece**. According to the peace treaty, all mainland regions and islands that took up arms against the Ottomans had the right to become part of the newly formed Greek state. However, the Ottomans probably considered the island of Samos too close to the **Asia Minor** mainland, so its union with Greece was not allowed. As a consolation, Samos was granted wide autonomy in 1834 as a semi-independent state under the supreme authority of the Turkish Sultan (interestingly, this island had some form of temporary local authority from the very beginning of the Greek rebellion in 1821, known as the Military-Political System of Samos).

The governance on the island of Samos, located only 1,200 metres from the **Turkish Aegean coast**, was carried out by a Christian prince appointed by the Sultan. All four inhabited settlements on the island had their own representatives in the Senate, while the Greek Orthodox Metropolitan presided over the 36-member parliament. Samos had its own flag and some form of military, while the Ottoman garrison had to leave the island.

A large number of princes governed Samos during its nearly 80 years of independence. The first prince was Stephanos Vogoridis, an Ottoman statesman of Bulgarian origin. He was known for renaming Vathy, the capital of Samos, to Stefanopolis in his honour (the old name was restored after his departure), but also for visiting the island only once during his reign. Ion Ghica was also one of the princes, who later served multiple times as the President of the Romanian Academy and the Prime Minister of **Romania**. Prince Đorđe Berović (in English: George Berovich; in Greek: Georgios Verovits; in Turkish: Beroviç Paşa), an Ottoman statesman of Serbian origin from the city of Scutari (Albanian: Shkodër; Serbian: Skadar) was also a popular ruler. The political standpoints of different princes varied, from those who were strongly pro-Greek, to those who advocated the independence of their island, and to those who sought deeper ties between Samos and the Ottoman palace.

Samos was a relatively developed state, so many Greeks from Asia Minor came to the free island in search of work. The state built numerous modern buildings in the capital, as well as a public transportation system, including a kind of tram. The production of olives, good quality wine, and tobacco brought significant profits to the state.

As a result of the favourable financial situation, elementary schools were built in all villages on the island, as well as several senior schools and colleges. From 1910, learning Esperanto was compulsory in all elementary and secondary schools of the Principality of Samos.

Just two years later, the Samos parliament declared unification with Greece, which also meant the end of learning Esperanto on the small island. It was the birthplace of the famous ancient Greek philosopher and mathematician Pythagoras, and the home of the goddess Hera, to whom one of the largest sanctuaries of ancient Greece, the Heraion of Samos, was dedicated.

REPUBLIC OF
SAN MARINO

Most serene ancient land of liberty

LOCATION: Apennine Peninsula
PERIOD: since 301 CE
AREA: 61 sq km
POPULATION: 33,660

The near-constant persecution of Christians in the Roman Empire throughout the late third and early fourth centuries changed only with the Edict of Milan, which was issued in 313 by the Roman co-emperors, Constantine the Great and Licinius, granting freedom of religion in the Empire. However, many Christians had sought refuge in more liberal parts of the Empire before that. One of them, Marinus, a stonemason from the island of Rab (in present-day Croatia), found refuge around the year 300 CE on the opposite coast of the Adriatic Sea in **Rimini** (in present-day **Italy**). Just a year later, Marinus moved to the nearby 750-metre-high Mt Titano, where he founded a monastery, which is considered to be the beginning of the state of San Marino. Marinus was later canonised, and the Republic of San Marino was named after him.

Today, San Marino is often considered one of the world's oldest republics, and its first constitution, from 1600, is still in effect, with amendments. The specificity of this state is its diarchy, a form of government in which power is vested in two rulers or authorities, known in the case of San Marino as Captains Regent. The co-rulers are elected for a term of six months, a tradition that dates to the mid-13th century. Despite the fact that stronger neighbours, especially the Papal State, occasionally and temporarily occupied the territory of the Republic, independence was always quickly restored, and San Marino's boundaries have been unchanged since the mid-15th century. Owing to the friendship of one regent with Napoleon, San Marino maintained its independence even during the French occupation of the rest of the Apennine Peninsula and much of Europe. In fact, Napoleon offered to expand San Marino, which the small republic politely declined for fear of later retaliation from aggrieved neighbours. San Marino remained neutral during most subsequent conflicts, including both World Wars, though during the Second World War, it accepted around 100,000 refugees from Italy, including a large number of Jews.

San Marino, known as the Most Serene Republic of San Marino, is only 10 kilometres away from the Adriatic Sea, but is completely surrounded by Italy, which has two enclaved states within it, San Marino and **Vatican City**, the most of any country.

Although it is not a European Union member, San Marino uses the euro as its currency, even minting coins with its national symbols. Its main sources of income are tourism, banking, agriculture, and the sale of postage stamps. In the capital, atop Mt Titano, there are three impressive towers, depicted on the state flag and coat of arms. The oldest and most famous among them was built in the 11th century, and a museum dedicated to St Marinus is found in the second-oldest tower. Due to special agreements with Italy, the production of all goods that are subject to government monopoly of the Republic of Italy, such as tobacco, are forbidden in San Marino. But San Marino gets by just fine, as a popular destination for global tourists and Italians alike, inducing everyone to enjoy its hilltop charm.

FREE STATE OF
SCHWENTEN

Free beer for 220 days

LOCATION: Western Poland
PERIOD: 1919
AREA: c. 50 sq km
POPULATION: c. 1,000

Poznań

Zielona Góra

SCHWENTEN
(Świętno)

Oder

POLAND

GERMANY

Wrocław

CZECHIA

0   50 km

The end of the First World War resulted in temporary turmoil: some states were collapsing, others were being created, and borders were changing with each passing day. For the Poles, this meant the re-establishment of an independent state, almost 125 years after the so-called Third Partition of Poland, when Prussia, **Austria**, and **Russia** divided the **Poland** of that time, among themselves, significantly reducing its size from the previous two partitions. However, the reappearance of Poland on the map of Europe meant the moving of **Germany**'s borders to the west, leaving a large number of ethnic Germans outside of their homeland. This was especially problematic in the area around the present-day city of Poznań, where the Greater Poland Uprising took place from the end of 1918 to the middle of 1919, when Polish forces attempted to seize as much territory as possible after the abdication of the German Emperor Wilhelm II, and the proclamation of the so-called Weimar Republic.

The village of Schwenten, located 70 kilometres southwest of Poznań, was predominantly inhabited by Germans. When the village leaders realised that there was a chance the Poles would attack and conquer the village, they tried to seek help from the nearby German garrison. However, due to the chaos which occurred in the German army after the abdication of the Emperor, this help was not obtained. Emil Hegemann, the church pastor in Schwenten, invoking the right to self-determination from the Fourteen Points of American President Woodrow Wilson, declared the Free State of Schwenten (German: Freistaat Schwenten) independent and neutral in relation to Germany and Poland.

Reverend Hegemann become the president and foreign minister of the newly created microstate. A parliament was elected, which appointed the forest warden as the minister of defence and the mayor as the minister of the interior. On the same day, a small, well-equipped army of 120 people was formed, and the government of the Free State abolished all obligations of its residents towards Germany.

Schwenten had an active foreign policy, which was implemented by President Hegemann. He managed to secure some form of recognition for his state from surrounding local Polish military leaders and from the Supreme People's Council, the organisation that led the Greater Poland Uprising. Border crossings were guarded around the clock, and for the approximately 220 days of its existence, Schwenten maintained international trade with its neighbours, Germany and Poland. The main local product was beer, which was not taxed by the state, so in return, members of the local parliament could enjoy free 'hop juice'.

Although the Free State of Schwenten was formally neutral, the almost exclusively German population still viewed their former homeland, Germany, with sympathy. When Emil Hegemann and the government of Schwenten realised that the surrounding Polish military units would likely use this as an excuse to attack and occupy their microstate, a decision was made, on 10 August 1919, to disband the Free State and become part of Germany. After the Second World War, the Germans were banished from Schwenten, and newly settled Poles officially renamed their village Świętno.

REPUBLIC OF
SENARICA

*Younger 'sister' of
the Republic of Venice*

LOCATION: Central Italy
PERIOD: mid-14th century – 1797
AREA: less than 10 sq km
POPULATION: c. 300

After the inhabitants of the small village of Senarica helped the Neapolitan Queen, Joanna I of Naples, to defeat the enemy army of the lord of the city of Milan in the mid-14th century, the Queen owed the villagers her thanks. She decided to grant them independence from the local nobility, and as a result, the independent Republic of Senarica (which most likely also included the neighbouring village of Poggio Umbricchio) was created.

Senarica had always been a relatively isolated village situated on the wooded mountain slopes of today's Gran Sasso and Monti della Laga National Park. Due to its extremely small size, the newly created Republic found an ally in the then-powerful **Republic of Venice**. This alliance also impacted the political life of Senarica: the head of state held the title of doge, just like in Venice, and the coat of arms featured a lion strangling a snake, inspired by the Venetian lion with wings. The Apennine micro-republic was obliged to send two soldiers to aid its 'big sister' in case of war. The local dialect also exhibited close ties with Venice, enriched with numerous words from the Venetian language, which the inhabitants of Senarica still use today in their everyday language.

The microstate produced a large quantity of chestnuts for food, as well as furniture and barrels made of chestnut wood. Its protection was entrusted to the Doge's guard, which played the role of a police force. However, this guard certainly could not match up to the powerful army of **Naples**, which appeared at the village entrance in 1797. That year, the Neapolitan King, Ferdinand IV, heard for the first time that there was a tiny republic within his kingdom whose inhabitants did not pay taxes, which he did not take kindly to. He ordered the army to occupy the village and abolish the Republic, which was achieved without any resistance, ending this microstate of just 300 inhabitants after 400 years in existence.

However, the real question is whether that microstate even existed at all? Solid evidence of the establishment of the independent Republic of Senarica has not been found (so far). The same goes for the documents concerning close ties with Venice or the election of local doges. The only clues are a few engraved inscriptions 'R. di Senarica' (from the Italian Repubblica di Senarica) on a couple of houses, as well as similar inscriptions on some old maps and numerous stories and legends. It is likely that the village did indeed enjoy some degree of autonomy, for example, it may have had the possibility of electing its local rulers and managing its local affairs independently to some extent. Such independent government of the citizens may have been called by the Latin term res publica ('public affair'), the same term from which the word 'republic' derives. Although Senarica was probably not an independent state in today's sense of the term, it seems that its inhabitants could have been proud of some freedoms barely imaginable to other people of that time.

PEOPLE'S REPUBLIC OF
TARNOBRZEG

The Red Priest and the peasants

LOCATION: Southeastern Poland
PERIOD: 1918–1919
AREA: c. 350 sq km
POPULATION: c. 77,000

POLAND

San

Vistula

Jezioro
Tarnobrzeskie

TARNOBRZEG

Nisko

0   20 km

The dissolution of Austria-Hungary following its defeat in the First World War led to complete chaos in areas where state authority disappeared. Such was the situation in the Kingdom of Galicia and Lodomeria, the poorest province of the Empire also known as Austrian Poland. In order to facilitate the peaceful unification of Galicia with the newly reborn **Poland**, the Polish members of the Austrian parliament established the Polish Liquidation Committee in late October 1918, with its seat in Kraków. Simultaneously, in their eastern neighbour, the Russian Revolution was taking place, which led to the overthrow of the monarchy and the victory of communism in **Russia**.

A priest and politician, Eugeniusz Okoń, took advantage of this turmoil. In November 1918, he led a group of local peasants to tear down the border posts between Galicia (still officially part of Austria-Hungary) and the Kingdom of Poland (a puppet state formed by **Germany** and Austria-Hungary from the Polish territory 'liberated' from Russia). In the following days, Okoń, along with his close associate Tomasz Dąbal, organised a series of political rallies of local peasants, who were opposed to both the former Austro-Hungary and the new temporary Polish authorities, comprising wealthy peasants and nobility. A large rally in the town of Tarnobrzeg, attended by more than 30,000 peasants, burdened by severe poverty prevailing in Galicia, was held on 6 November 1918. After a fiery speech against the faltering Austro-Hungarian Empire and the local nobility, Okoń proclaimed the rule of the people, effectively initiating the period of the People's Republic of Tarnobrzeg, a microstate at the confluence of the San and Vistula rivers. Although Tarnobrzeg formally acknowledged the authority of the Committee in Kraków, all real power lay in the hands of the peasants, who made all political decisions at weekly rallies, held by the monument of Bartosz Głowacki, one of the leaders of the Polish peasant army during the Kościuszko Uprising of 1794. Tomasz Dąbal was declared president of the new Soviet-style state, which immediately established its own military-police force, the Rural Guard. However, the Guard made little effort to protect the estates of wealthy landowners or the shops and taverns of local Jews, which were regular targets for looting.

Such behaviour by the Soviet mini-state did not go unnoticed by the Committee in Kraków, the representative of the emerging new Polish state. In December 1918, the Committee sent out military units whose task was to disarm the peasants throughout the Republic of Tarnobrzeg, but they had little success. Soon after, the provisional Polish authorities from Warsaw called for elections for the entire territory of the new state. Okoń and Dąbal ran in the elections, spreading their radical communist ideas among the peasants and poor workers. This gave the prosecutor cause to order their arrest. Dąbal managed to escape, but Okoń was arrested on 6 January 1919, which marked the end of the Republic of Tarnobrzeg. However, their political list won nearly 90% of the votes in the territory of the former microstate, enabling them to enter parliament, therefore receiving immunity and release from prison. The 'Red Priest', as Okoń was known, became a very active member of the Polish parliament, where he continued to passionately advocate his strong leftist views from the time of the Republic of Tarnobrzeg.

PRINCIPALITY OF
THEODORO

The last moments of the Roman Empire

LOCATION: Crimean Peninsula
PERIOD: early 14th century–1475
AREA: 1,400 sq km
POPULATION: C. 200,000

According to legend, Rome was founded in 753 BCE. Constantinople, the capital of the Eastern Roman (Byzantine) Empire, fell in 1453 to the powerful attacks of the **Ottoman Empire**. For most people, this marks the end of the Roman state. However, experts in history know that the Roman tradition persisted in the Empire of Trebizond until 1461 when the Ottomans finally conquered this small remnant of the **Byzantine Empire** on the present-day Black Sea coast of Turkey. But this was not the last of it. Traces of the Roman state survived for another 14 years on the northern coast of the Black Sea, on the Crimean Peninsula.

The population of **Crimea** was composed of a mixture of Greeks (the first Greek colonies were formed as early as the 7th century BCE), Crimean Goths, Alans, Cumans, and numerous other ethnic groups. Over time, this blend of people mostly adopted the Greek language and the Orthodox religion. After the Crusader conquest of Constantinople in 1204, the southern half of the peninsula politically became a vassal of the Empire of Trebizond, which emerged from the ruins of the Byzantine Empire. In the first half of the 13th century, the Mongols conquered most of Crimea, but the southern part retained its partial independence, with regular tribute payments to the new overlords.

At the beginning of the 14th century, southern Crimea was first mentioned in historical sources as the Principality of Gothia. The name is thought to be the result of a large number of Germanic Goths who inhabited the peninsula, although the actual ethnic makeup of the Principality at this time is contested by historians.

The capital of the nowadays little-known Gothia was Theodoro (also known as Manhup or Mangup), a fortified city located on a high plateau in inland Crimea. Soon, the entire state was named after its capital, and the title of its ruler from the beginning of the 15th century was 'Lord of the city of Theodoro and the Maritime Region'. Theodoro suffered a heavy blow in 1395 when the mighty Tamerlane destroyed the capital and captured the entire principality. The death of this Mongol ruler in 1404 brought the semi-independence of Theodoro again, and it became a significant trading power in the Black Sea.

A new threat, in the form of the powerful Ottoman Empire, cast a shadow over the whole of Crimea in the second half of the 15th century. The son-in-law of the last ruler of Theodoro, Stephen the Great, ruler of **Moldavia**, sent military aid to his relatives, but it was not enough. After a three-month siege, the Ottomans captured the fortified city. Members of the ruling family suffered greatly: the Prince was killed; his wife and daughters were assigned to the Sultan's harem; and his son was forcibly converted to Islam. Despite this, Greek religious institutions continued to function, just as the use of the Greek language persisted until modern times.

Rome wasn't built in a day, but its state, political, and cultural tradition lasted an impressive 2,228 years, from the founding of the city in 753 BCE to the fall of the Principality of Theodoro in 1475 CE.

One of the gates of the 'God-guarded fortress of Theodoro', according to the inscription found on the walls.

A modern welcome to the Free Territory of Trieste on Piazza della Borsa, one of the main squares in Trieste, Italy.

FREE TERRITORY OF
TRIESTE

Two zones, one free territory

LOCATION: Northern coast of the Adriatic Sea
PERIOD: 1947–1954
AREA: 738 sq km
POPULATION: c. 330,000

ITALY

SLOVENIA

Zone A

ADRIATIC SEA

TRIESTE

Koper/Capodistria

Zone B

Zone B

CROATIA

Novigrad

0   20 km

Italy's participation in the First World War on the side of the Allies brought significant territorial gains to the country at the expense of the dissolved Austro-Hungarian Empire, including the Julian March and the Istrian Peninsula, with the cities of Trieste, Gorizia, Pula, and Rijeka, among others. The Second World War brought many changes to that situation, as Italy participated on the side of the Axis powers and, as a defeated nation, suffered numerous territorial losses. Among other territories, it had to cede a large part of the Julian March and Istria to the new communist Yugoslavia. However, who would get the city of Trieste and the northern part of Istria was not as easily decided.

Since the Allies did not want the conflict to continue, they decided in 1947 that this disputed area would become the Free Territory of Trieste, a microstate under the control of the United Nations Security Council. Although formally regarded as a single territory, it was politically and economically divided into two areas: Zone A included the city of Trieste and the coastal strip to the north of it; and Zone B consisted of the northwestern part of the Istrian Peninsula. The population of the entire Territory comprised Italians (mostly in urban areas and the narrow coastal strip) and Slovenes and Croats (mainly in villages and inland), and a smaller number of Jews, Greeks, Albanians, and Istro-Romanians. The official languages were Italian and Slovenian, while in Zone B, Serbo-Croatian was also used unofficially.

The combination of split administration – Zone A under the **United States** and the **United Kingdom**, Zone B under socialist Yugoslavia – and the fact that the Cold War began almost immediately after the end of the Second World War, resulted in joint government bodies of the Free Territory not being formed, these primarily being the election of a governor and parliament. Instead, both zones were under military administration, which meant that Trieste never became a functioning unified state, despite having the legal status, and even issuing its own currency and postage stamps. The only elections that took place were municipal elections, in 1949 and 1952.

The main sources of income were two important ports, the Port of Koper/Capodistria and the Free Port of Trieste. What is peculiar about the port of Trieste is that its status as a free zone (often referred to as 'offshore') was granted as early as 1719 by Charles VI, the Holy Roman Emperor. This status was later confirmed by the Treaty of Peace with Italy in 1947 (the same treaty that established the Free Territory of Trieste). Today, the Port of Trieste still holds the status of a free port within Italy and the EU, which provides numerous benefits for companies operating there.

In 1954, the US, UK, Italy, and Yugoslavia signed the London Memorandum, which disestablished the Free Territory of Trieste, handing over Zone A to Italy and Zone B to Yugoslavia. The border between Yugoslavia and Italy was definitively confirmed only in 1975 by the Treaty of Osimo. Some organisations in Trieste still believe that the Territory was illegally dissolved and advocate for the separation of Trieste from Italy, and the re-establishment of the Free Territory of Trieste (at least its Zone A) as a sovereign microstate between **Slovenia** and Italy.

VATICAN CITY STATE

Small state, enormous influence

LOCATION: Rome, Italy
PERIOD: since 1929
AREA: 0.44 sq km
POPULATION: c. 760

0   30 km

In the very heart of the former **Roman Empire**, in the ancient capital of Rome, is the smallest sovereign state possibly of all time: the Vatican City. Numerous religious and cultural landmarks of exceptional importance are located within this small area. Some of these sites include St Peter's Basilica; the Sistine Chapel, where the new pope is traditionally elected and where priceless frescoes can be found, such as Michelangelo's *The Last Judgment*; the Vatican Museum, with hundreds of Roman sculptures and works by Renaissance masters; and the Vatican Library, one of the oldest in the world, with an exceptional collection of religious, historical, and other texts.

The Vatican can be perceived as the successor to the former Papal State, which existed for more than 1,000 years, from 756 to 1870. During the unification of numerous small states on the Apennine Peninsula and the creation of the Kingdom of Italy, the territory of the Papal State was conquered by military force and annexed to the new **Italy**, while the Pope retreated to the Vatican. Almost 60 years later, in 1929, Italy and the Holy See signed the Lateran Treaty, by which the small area of the Vatican City gained independence and became the sovereign seat of the Pope and the entire Catholic Church.

The Holy See ('See' derives from the Latin word *sedes*, meaning 'seat') represents the supreme body that governs the Catholic Church. Although the terms 'Vatican' and 'Holy See' are often considered synonymous, they are not. The Holy See and its sovereignty have existed with or without a specific territory since the time of the Roman Empire. The 'task' of the Vatican since its establishment in 1929 has been to provide the Holy See with a location for its civil authority. Diplomatic relations with almost all countries in the world are maintained by the Holy See, not the Vatican.

Today, the Vatican is a theocracy (a form of governance where religious structure dominates the state) and an absolute elective monarchy, in which the Pope exercises principal legislative, executive, and judicial powers. This makes him the only absolute monarch in Europe, with broader powers even than the prince of **Liechtenstein** (although the princes of Liechtenstein have hereditary authority).

In addition to the Vatican as its sovereign territory, the Holy See also possesses numerous properties in and around Rome, which enjoy extraterritorial status, meaning they belong to Italy but Italian authorities have no control over them without the permission of the Holy See. The economy of the Vatican is based on tourism and donations from worshippers, and Vatican postage stamps and euro coins are highly sought after by collectors. The colourful uniforms of the Swiss Guard, a small military unit responsible for the personal security of the Pope, are a particular attraction for tourists.

Despite its small size and harmonious existence within its encompassing neighbour, the Vatican has a border dispute with Italy. This concerns a narrow strip, 3 metres wide and approximately 70 metres long, known as the Curl of Italy (Italian: Ricciolo d'Italia), which has been disputed since the formation of the smallest state in the world.

AFRICA

The town of Phuthaditjhaba in South Africa served as the capital of the former Qwaqwa Bantustan during the apartheid era.

STATE OF **ANJOUAN**

Volcanic land of coups d'état

LOCATION: Indian Ocean
PERIOD: 1997–2002, 2007–2008
AREA: 425 sq km
POPULATION: C. 300,000

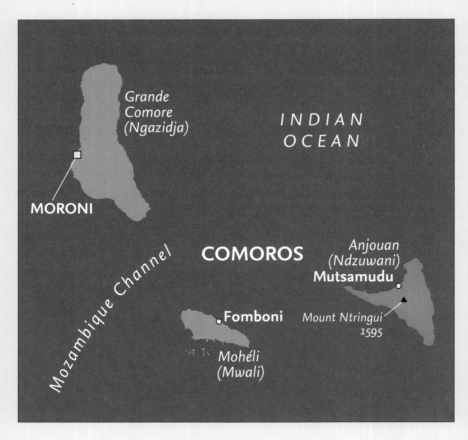

Grande Comore (Ngazidja)

INDIAN OCEAN

MORONI

Mozambique Channel

COMOROS

Anjouan (Ndzuwani)
Mutsamudu

Fomboni

Mount Ntringui 1595

Mohéli (Mwali)

0   50 km

The Comoro Archipelago is located in the Mozambique Channel between the northern tip of **Madagascar** and the African mainland. Until 1974, the entire archipelago was a French colony. In that year, a referendum on independence was held; the island of Mayotte (known in Comorian as Maore) decided to remain part of France and is now a French overseas department. The remaining three islands – Grande Comore (Ngazidja), Anjouan (Ndzuwani), and Mohéli (Mwali) – formed the state of **Comoros**. Unfortunately, independence brought Comoros constant instability and numerous coups, almost one per year in the first 30 years of independence, the first occurring just one month after it was declared. The political system and the name of the country were changed several times; the State of Comoros soon became the Federal Islamic Republic of Comoros and is now called the Union of the Comoros. The predominantly Muslim population comprises Bantu people, Arabs, Malays, and people from nearby Madagascar. The official languages are Comorian (Shikomor), French and Arabic.

The unstable situation led to frequent demands for greater autonomy from the two smaller islands, Anjouan and Mohéli. In mid-July 1997, separatist demonstrations were held on Anjouan, during which two people were killed. Several days later, whilst the governor was on a business trip, supporters of the island's independence took advantage of his absence and declared the reintegration of Anjouan under French rule. Soon afterwards, a nearly identical process occurred on the island of Mohéli, and French flags were raised on both islands. However, not willing to strain relations with Comoros and the Organization of African Unity, France simply did not respond to these offers from the islanders. The island of Mohéli returned to Comoros the following year.

When the separatist authorities realised that **France** would not accept them under its auspices, they declared the sovereign State of Anjouan. In the referendum held to confirm the will of the people, 99% of the voters supported independence. The following year, Anjouan adopted its new constitution. The state of instability and frequent coups d'état continued in the newly formed state.

However, in 2002, the authorities of Comoros proposed the formation of a new state union comprising the three islands with broad autonomy, under the name Union of the Comoros. The President of Anjouan, Mohamed Bacar, accepted the new Union, but in 2007, at the end of his five-year mandate, he refused to step down from power, initiating a new conflict with the central authorities. That same year, Anjouan once again withdrew from the Comorian state and declared independence. This time, the Union of the Comoros did not accept Anjouan's declaration of independence and decided on military action against the island. On 25 March 2008, the Comorian forces, reinforced by African Union soldiers, began the invasion of Anjouan. One day later, the entire island was under the control of the Comorian army.

The new authorities of Anjouan decided to repair relations with the Union of the Comoros. One of the steps on this path was the adoption of a new flag, which would feature the main symbol from the Comoros flag, the Muslim crescent moon, and four stars representing the four islands of the archipelago.

KINGDOM OF
BENI ABBAS

A Berber* heartland in the mountains

LOCATION: Algeria
PERIOD: 1510–1872
AREA: a few hundred square km
POPULATION: C. 100,000

* The term 'Berber' is now considered pejorative and the people prefer to be known as Amazigh instead. What was known as the Berber language is now referred to as the Amazigh (Tamazight) language.

0   500 km

In the early 8th century, the unstoppable power of the Umayyad Caliphate conquered the lands from the Indus River to the Atlantic Ocean, including almost the entire Iberian Peninsula. Just a few years after the conquest of this vast peninsula, near the northern coast of present-day Spain, the Battle of Covadonga took place in a narrow strip ruled by local Christian rulers. The result of the battle was the victory of the Christian Visigoth Prince Pelagius and the founding of the Kingdom of Asturias, which eventually became **Spain** and **Portugal**. The struggle of Christian states against the Muslim Caliphate lasted until 1492, when the Christians conquered Granada, the last remaining part of the former Umayyad Caliphate on the Iberian Peninsula. The Spaniards then continued their conquest of North Africa, capturing Bejaïa in 1510, an important port on the Algerian coast, and the former capital of the same-named Emirate of Bejaïa.

The Berber population of the Emirate then retreated to the mountainous areas several tens of kilometres south of the coast, which was ruled by the Spaniards. There, in the high Bibans mountains, they founded their new capital, Kalâa ('citadel') of Ait Abbas (in Berber*) or Beni Abbas (in Arabic), an inaccessible fortification on a heart-shaped rocky plateau at an altitude of nearly 1,000 metres. The area around the city became known as the kingdom of the same name. Although relatively small, the Kingdom became known as a fortification against Spanish advances, as well as later against the Regency of Algiers, a semi-independent territory under the supreme authority of the **Ottoman Empire**. At one point, the city had 80,000 inhabitants, many of whom were Muslims and Jews who had fled from Spain after the fall of Muslim rule. Periodically, an army of about 10,000 soldiers expanded the Kingdom's rule southward towards the Sahara, but it was mostly concentrated in the areas around the fortified capital, where it successfully repelled attacks several times from Ottoman **Algeria**.

Despite frequent battles, culture flourished in Kalâa, and the city was prestigious in terms of cultural and intellectual activities. The buildings in the city, as well as in the surrounding villages, were beautiful, spacious, and modern, which was unusual for other Berber lands. Olives, figs, grapes, and prickly pears were grown on the fertile plateau of Medjana near the capital, and sheep were bred for meat and wool.

Beni Abbas was ruled by the Mokrani dynasty, a powerful Kabyle family (Kabyles are a Berber ethnic group from Kabylia, the region between the Biban range and the Mediterranean Sea). The rulers typically used titles such as sultan, sheikh, and even caliph.

The arrival of the French in the 19th century and the beginning of the colonisation of North Africa brought great danger to the small Berber state. At first, the rulers of Beni Abbas maintained relatively friendly relations with their new French neighbours, retaining a semi-independent status. However, this changed when the Kabyles rose up in arms against the colonial rulers. The superior French army quickly suppressed the rebellion, and the previously nearly unconquerable Kalâa surrendered on 22 July 1871, as one of the last strongholds against invaders, and as one of the last independent Kabyle/Berber states.

CHRISTIAN
BERBER* KINGDOMS

A fractured empire

LOCATION: North Africa
PERIOD: 6th–8th century
AREA: a few hundred square km
POPULATION: unknown

* The term 'Berber' is now considered pejorative and the people prefer to be known as Amazigh instead.
  What was known as the Berber language is now referred to as the Amazigh (Tamazight) language.

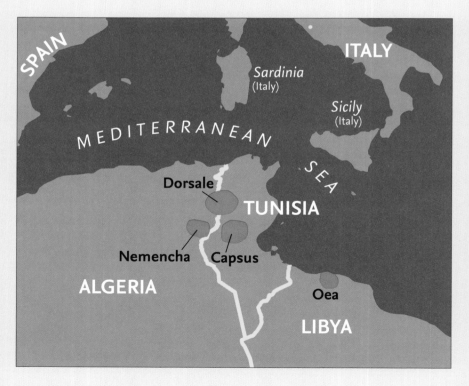

0   500 km

The constant attacks from Germanic and other tribes on the Apennine Peninsula during the 5th century led to the weakening of imperial control over the provinces of the Western Roman Empire. The migration of the Germanic Vandals and their Iranian allies, the Alans, from the Iberian Peninsula to North Africa in 429 CE, and the subsequent conquest of Carthage ten years later, resulted in the isolation of the Roman province of Mauretania Caesariensis (approximately present-day northern **Algeria**) from the rest of the Empire. This province was inhabited by Berbers (Moors) and Romans, who defended themselves from the newly created Vandal state. Thus, in the early 6th century, the Mauro-Roman Kingdom was established – a state of Christian Berbers who mainly followed Roman traditions. However, Emperor Justinian I overthrew the Vandal state in the first half of the 6th century, and re-established Roman rule in Carthage and North Africa. The Mauro-Roman Kingdom fragmented into a number of smaller states. The **Roman Empire** granted them autonomy so they could be allies, while showering the rulers of these small states with gifts.

The newly formed Berber microstates were:

- The Kingdom of Oea (in present-day Tripoli, Libya), known for King Cabaon and his great victory over the previously dominant army of the Vandal Kingdom. This victory in 523 CE marked the end of Vandal rule over the region of Tripolitania and its cities of Oea, Sabratha, and Leptis Magna. After King Cabaon, this state slowly fell into obscurity.
- The Kingdom of Capsus, a small and not very significant Berber state, occupied a small territory around its capital city, Capsa (present-day Gafsa, **Tunisia**). Many historians believe that this was precisely the place where the African Latin language, now extinct, was spoken the longest, and that a large number of inhabitants were of the Christian faith until the 13th century. This region is also known for the ancient Capsian culture from the period 10,000 to 6,000 BCE. Members of this culture were known as 'snail eaters' (snails were a significant part of their diet, as evidenced by great middens of snail shells from that time), and it is believed that they were the ancestors of all Berbers of North Africa.
- The Kingdom of Dorsale was a coalition of several Berber tribes, led by Antales, leader of the Frexes tribe. The centre of this state was located in the city of Thala, in present-day Tunisia, not far from the border with Algeria. This location was chosen because of its high altitude (about 1,000 metres), which gave it natural fortification, and an additional advantage of a cooler climate.
- The Kingdom of Nemencha, near Capsus and Dorsale, was a small and isolated Berber state that, owing to its location, long avoided being involved in the war conflicts between the Berbers, Vandals, and Byzantium.

All the small Berber states of North Africa experienced the same fate: they were conquered by the rapidly expanding Umayyad Caliphate, which took over the whole of North Africa in the early 8th century. Berber tribes soon accepted Islam, but retain their language and traditions still to this day.

REPUBLIC OF
KLEIN VRYSTAAT

*Farming land
acquired by deceit*

LOCATION: South Africa
PERIOD: 1886–1891
AREA: c. 150 sq km
POPULATION: 72

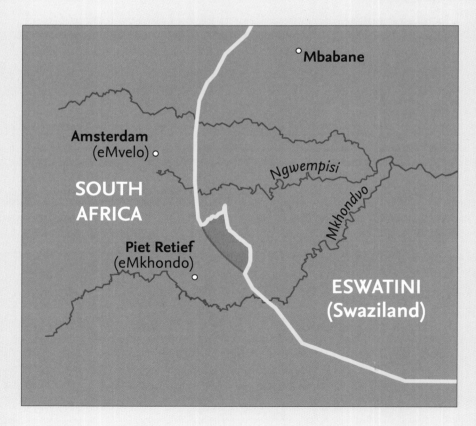

After the Dutch conquest of some parts of **South Africa**, the first settlers, known as the Boers (from the Dutch, meaning 'farmers'), began to settle in Kaapkolonie (Cape Colony) in the 17th century. Sometime after that, the Boers started migrating, some voluntarily and some under pressure from the British, into the interior of present-day South Africa, where they eventually established several so-called 'Boer republics'. The two largest ones, the South African Republic (Transvaal) and the Orange Free State, received widespread international recognition. However, in addition to these, there were a dozen or so smaller republics under Boer control, created from a mix of settlers from the **Netherlands**, **France**, **Germany**, and other countries.

One of the smallest Boer republics was called Klein Vrystaat (sometimes written as Kleinvrijstaat Republiek), which in Dutch means Little Free State. The foundation for the establishment of this microstate was laid in 1876, when a small group of Boers, led by General Joachim Johannes Ferreira, settled on land they had purchased from Mbandzeni Dlamini IV, the King of Swaziland (now **Eswatini**). The illiterate King was, in this case, a victim of deceit: although he was told he was signing a temporary lease for land use, what he actually signed was a permanent licence for settlers to inhabit 15,000 hectares of land along the border with the Transvaal. The Boers built several small farms on this land, and the King was forced to allow them to establish their own self-government.

The Boers were not content with self-government, so in 1886, they declared the independence of their territory, which they named Klein Vrystaat. At the same time, they adopted a constitution, and formed a government. The flag of the neighbouring Transvaal was chosen (the so-called Vierkleur, 'four colours') but with one barely noticeable modification: the vertical green field was slightly narrower than on the Transvaal flag. King Mbandzeni tried to force the Boers out, claiming they had violated the terms of the agreement, but he did not succeed. Thus, a small free state was created, with fewer than 100 people living on its 150 square kilometres. The state was governed by three eminent persons who formed a triumvirate, a kind of political institution, which is also mentioned on the official seal of Klein Vrystaat (Dutch: *Onder het bestuur van de Driemanschap*; English: Under the rule of the Triumvirate).

Such a small state certainly could not survive for long, so the local leaders sent a request to the government of the South African Republic (Transvaal) to incorporate them. The request was accepted on 11 April 1891, when the smallest Boer republic officially became part of the largest one. In 1902, the British conquered all Boer republics, laying the basis for the creation of today's multi-ethnic **South Africa**. The last testimony of the existence of the former Little Free State is the 'bite', whereby present-day South Africa 'bit off' a piece of what was then Swaziland territory near the town of Piet Retief/eMkhondo.

QWAQWA BANTUSTAN

Apartheid's smallest microstate

LOCATION: South Africa
PERIOD: 1974–1994
AREA: 655 sq km
POPULATION: C. 200,000

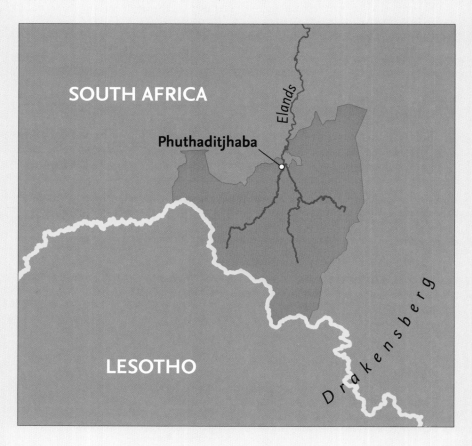

0   20 km

In 1959, during apartheid in **South Africa**, and **Namibia** (then under the administration of South Africa), the authorities of South Africa decided to create Bantustans, or homelands, a kind of reserve for their Black populations. Ten Bantustans were formed in South Africa and Namibia (then known as South West Africa). Four Bantustans eventually gained formal independence from South Africa, while others had (formal) broad autonomy, with a plan to gain independence later. The unilateral formation of Bantustans, accompanied by violent resettlement of the Black population from other parts of South Africa, was never recognised by the UN or any other state. According to the 1970 law, the Black population was forced to take citizenship of the Bantustan designated for the ethnic group from which the individuals originated, while South African citizenship was automatically revoked. Almost half of South Africa's population lived in Bantustans, and the size of individual Bantustans varied significantly – from the largest, Transkei, with an impressive 43,000 square kilometres, to the microstate, Qwaqwa, with an area of about 655 square kilometres.

Qwaqwa was the smallest Bantustan, intended to be the homeland for around 200,000 members of the Basotho people, an ethnic group that was a part of the majority population in the enclave-state of **Lesotho**. Therefore, a small region along the northeastern border with Lesotho was designated as the location for this Bantustan. The Bantustan, which may have been named after the frequent snowfalls on the peaks of the nearby Drakensburg mountains ('qwa-qwa' meaning 'whiter than white'), gained self-government in 1974. The area of this microstate was small but elevated, sitting between 1,500 and 3,000 metres above sea level.

The local authorities of Qwaqwa were responsible for transportation, education, agriculture, and healthcare, and the region officially had the status of a self-governing state within South Africa. In the 1975 elections, Kenneth Mopeli was elected as Chief Minister, and he spent a significant part of his mandate seeking the territorial expansion of his Bantustan, which South Africa approved several times, though only to a small extent. Additionally, Mopeli's government focused on building a large number of schools (primary education became compulsory and free), and during that time, the University of Qwaqwa was established. English and Afrikaans were taught in schools, but the only official language of this Bantustan was Sesotho.

The economy of the small pseudo state largely depended on the income of seasonal workers, who worked in South Africa, as well as on poorly developed agriculture and industry. The development of tourism was also initiated, although financial problems and poor infrastructure hindered all major projects.

When the first democratic constitution was adopted by South Africa in 1994, the apartheid system was abolished, along with all Bantustans. Thus, after 20 years, Qwaqwa lost its self-government, having never achieved independence. Today it is part of the Free State province, which was called Orange Free State until 1994. A large part of the territory of the former Bantustan is now the QwaQwa National Park, a part of the larger Golden Gate Highlands National Park.

ISLANDS OF
REFRESHMENT

Prince of potatoes and Lord of seal skins

LOCATION: South Atlantic Ocean
PERIOD: 1811–1816
AREA: c. 115 sq km
POPULATION: 4

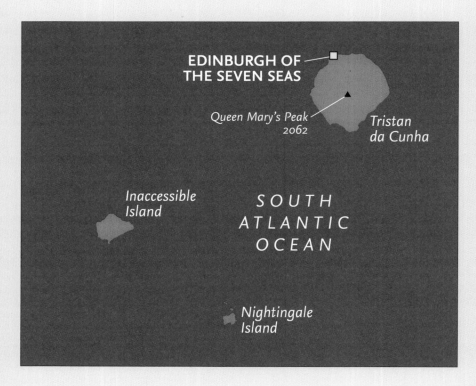

EDINBURGH OF
THE SEVEN SEAS

Queen Mary's Peak
2062

Tristan
da Cunha

Inaccessible
Island

*SOUTH
ATLANTIC
OCEAN*

Nightingale
Island

0   20 km

Tristan da Cunha is a small, isolated archipelago situated in the middle of the South Atlantic Ocean, approximately 2,800 kilometres from Cape Town, **South Africa**, and about 3,250 kilometres from Rio de Janeiro, **Brazil**. Due to such great distance from neighbouring continents, the archipelago was uninhabited until modern times, and even exploration ships of major maritime powers in the 18th and 19th centuries rarely visited this remote place.

The first permanent inhabitants, Jonathan Lambert from Salem, Massachusetts, and his two shipmates, landed on the archipelago in the last days of 1810. Shortly afterwards, another man joined them. These former pirates endeavoured to grow vegetables, primarily potatoes, and sell them to ships passing by the island. In addition to fruit saplings and various vegetable seeds, they also brought a large number of poultry and pigs, and they hunted seals, selling their oil to passing ships.

A month into this business venture, on 4 February 1811, Jonathan Lambert issued a proclamation declaring the islands of Tristan da Cunha as his independent state. He gave the proclamation to the crew of a passing ship, who handed it over to newspapers in Boston, where it was published on 18 July 1811. Lambert gave himself the title of Lord and Prince in this proclamation, and renamed the archipelago and the largest island, as the 'Islands of Refreshment'. He also renamed two smaller islands under his claimed authority: Inaccessible Island to Pintard Island, and Nightingale Island to Lovel Island. At the same time, he named the settlement where his residence was located 'Reception' and bestowed his subjects with a new flag. Allegedly, he sent the Proclamation of Independence to all European governments.

The British government, which at that time had not yet officially annexed the islands of Tristan da Cunha, was not thrilled with the emergence of this microstate. However, Napoleon's campaigns across Europe prevented the dispatch of a military ship that could have annexed the archipelago to the **United Kingdom**, allowing Lord and Prince Lambert's rule to continue.

As the profits from potatoes and other vegetables were not sufficient, the ruler of the Islands of Refreshment attempted to arrange the export of seal skins and oil, which were abundant on the cold beaches of Tristan da Cunha. This endeavour might have been successful if Prince Lambert had lived long enough. In mid-May 1812, he set sail in a small boat with two of his three subjects to fish and investigate a wreck brought in by ocean currents. All three men drowned, leaving the remaining inhabitant of the island, an Italian named Tomasso Corri, alone for months until two new men joined him, with whom he continued to engage in agriculture.

Four years later, on 14 August 1816, the British government officially annexed these remote islands, thereby finally abolishing the microstate in the middle of the Atlantic. The archipelago, home to approximately 250 people today, is now part of the United Kingdom Overseas Territory of St Helena, Ascension and Tristan da Cunha, and the capital and only settlement of Tristan da Cunha is called Edinburgh of the Seven Seas.

REPUBLIC OF **SALÉ**

A pirate republic trading from Morocco to Bristol

LOCATION: Morocco
PERIOD: 1627–1668
AREA: c. 1 sq km
POPULATION: C. 20,000

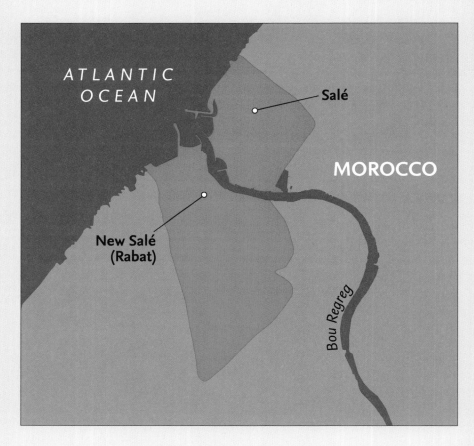

ATLANTIC
OCEAN

Salé

MOROCCO

New Salé
(Rabat)

Bou Regreg

0   2 km

The Reconquista, the struggle of Christian rulers to expel Muslims (known as Moors) from **Spain** and **Portugal**, lasted from the 8th to the end of the 15th century. After the final Christian victory and a brief period of religious freedom in Spain, many Muslims were expelled to North Africa. In the early 17th century, almost 20,000 Moriscos (as people of Moorish descent were called) abandoned the town of Hornachos in southwestern Spain and found their new home in the deserted city of Salé, in present-day **Morocco**.

Salé is located on the northern coast of the Bou Regreg River estuary. On the opposite coast lies the present-day capital of Morocco, Rabat, known in the 17th century as New Salé. The two cities, populated by wealthy refugees from Spain, united and formed the semi-independent city-state of Salé in 1614 under the supreme authority of the Saadi Sultanate, the predecessor of modern-day Morocco. This small state became the base of the 'Salé Rovers', pirates who raided Spanish and other European ships, as well as coastal settlements throughout Western and Southern Europe. During such attacks, numerous Christians were captured and sold into slavery or held for ransom. Some captured Christians remained among their abductors, converted to Islam, and often rose in the pirate hierarchy. A notable example was Jan Janszoon, a Dutchman, who under his new Muslim name, Reis Murad, served as the Grand Admiral of Salé from 1619 to 1627. One of his greatest achievements was the five-year occupation of the English island of Lundy, located in the **Bristol Channel**. This small island served as an excellent base for attacks on ships sailing to or from Bristol, while simultaneously serving as temporary accommodation for kidnapped Europeans before they were enslaved in Salé.

As Salé became wealthier, its inhabitants decided to expel the Sultan's governor in 1627 and declare an independent microstate of the Republic of Salé, also known as the Bou Regreg Republic or the Republic of the Two Banks. The Republic ceased to recognise the supreme authority of the Sultan, and refused to pay him taxes on pirated loot. The small but powerful pirate state was ruled by a council (or 'diwan'), which elected the governor and military commander. As most of the population and council members at that time were from the city of Hornachos or the region of **Andalusia**, Spanish was the official language of the documents of the Republic of Salé.

Despite constant pirate attacks on Spanish ships, Salé's connection with Spain remained strong, insomuch that in 1631, the Hornacheros, the inhabitants of Salé originating from Hornachos, offered their Republic to the Spanish king. Although negotiations were initiated, they didn't get very far, due to internal conflicts between the Hornacheros and Andalusians. These conflicts weakened the position of the micro-republic, leading to increasing external influence, and resulting in Salé becoming a sort of protectorate of the powerful Berber tribe, the Dilaites, from 1640. The final end of the Republic of Salé came in 1668 when a Sultan from the Alawite dynasty, which still rules Morocco today, defeated the Dilaites and abolished the independence of the pirate microstate.

DEMOCRATIC REPUBLIC OF
SÃO TOMÉ AND PRÍNCIPE

Equatorial centre of the slave trade

LOCATION: Gulf of Guinea, Central Africa
PERIOD: since 1975
AREA: 964 sq km
POPULATION: 227,380

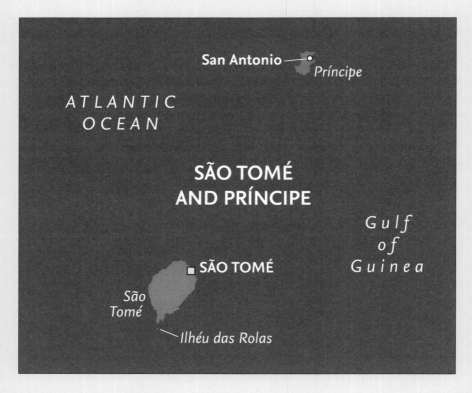

San Antonio — Príncipe

ATLANTIC OCEAN

SÃO TOMÉ AND PRÍNCIPE

Gulf of Guinea

SÃO TOMÉ

São Tomé

Ilhéu das Rolas

0   50 km

The island nation of **São Tomé and Príncipe** is located on islands of the same name in the Gulf of Guinea. The Equator passes through the southern islet of Ilhéu das Rolas (also known as Ilhéu Gago Coutinho). Although scientists claim that this small archipelago was formed around 30 million years ago as part of a volcanic chain along the **Cameroon** line, stretching from Lake Chad to the small island of Annobón, it seems that the first people set foot on the islands only at the end of the 15th century. They were discovered by Portuguese explorers who claimed them in the name of their kingdom. The first settlements were established in the late 15th century, and sugarcane plantations were started. At first, the main workers on these plantations were convicts and Jews, including children as young as eight years old, who arrived on São Tomé and Príncipe from **Portugal** as part of a forced Catholicisation programme. Later, this arduous work was done by enslaved people, primarily brought from the nearby Kingdom of Kongo (a former kingdom of central Africa). Favourable climate and fertile volcanic soil made São Tomé the main sugar producer during the 16th century. Later on, other countries took over that primacy, and São Tomé slowly became a centre of the trade in enslaved people. In the 19th century, new large coffee and cocoa plantations were initiated.

São Tomé and Príncipe remained a Portuguese colony until 1974 when leftist members of the Portuguese army overthrew the conservative and autocratic rule of the so-called Second Portuguese Republic. The new government granted independence to most colonies, and São Tomé and Príncipe declared independence on 12 July 1975. Fifteen years later, the island microstate adopted a democratic constitution, through which it became one of the most stable and freest African countries, with freedom of speech and political freedoms respected.

Nowadays, the main economic activities on the islands are agriculture (production of cocoa, coffee, and copra), fishing, and light industry. The production of oil is gaining significance, as well as tourism, which is supported by large foreign investments.

The ties with the former colonial state still remain very strong and are reflected in the interconnected economy, culture, and education, as well as in the defence of the archipelago against modern-day pirates. The official language is Portuguese, although several variants of Portuguese-Creole languages are widely spoken. Almost 90% of the population lives on the largest island, São Tomé, while only about 10,000 live on the smaller island, Príncipe, which has the official status of an autonomous region with its own parliament and government.

Both islands are known for their lush forests, diverse wildlife, and beautiful beaches. The Parque Natural Obô de São Tomé, a dense and biologically important forest, covers a large part of the island of São Tomé. Within this forest lies Pico Cão Grande, an impressive needle-shaped lava peak standing 370 metres high over the surrounding terrain. Climbing this peak is still considered very challenging and dangerous, primarily because of slippery moss-covered rocks and a large number of snakes. Therefore, it's not surprising that Pico Cão Grande (Great Dog Peak, in English) was successfully conquered for the first time only in 1991.

*Pico Cão Grande, an iconic landmark
in Parque Natural Obô de São Tomé,
São Tomé and Príncipe.*

Aldabra giant tortoise on the beach of Praslin island, Seychelles.

REPUBLIC OF
SEYCHELLES

Reclaimed from colonial states and the sea

LOCATION: Indian Ocean
PERIOD: since 1976
AREA: 457 sq km
POPULATION: 100,000

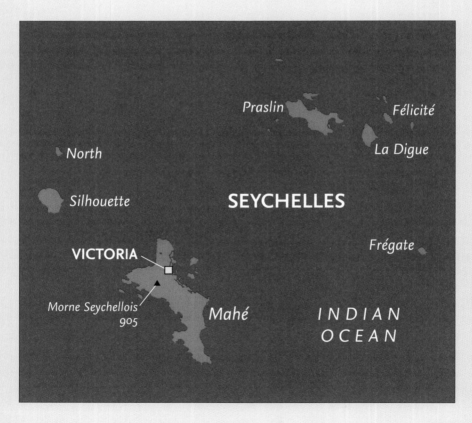

North

Praslin

Félicité

La Digue

Silhouette

SEYCHELLES

VICTORIA

Frégate

Morne Seychellois
905

Mahé

INDIAN
OCEAN

0   25 km

Seychelles, officially Republic of Seychelles (or Repibilik Sesel in Seychellois Creole), is the smallest African country, both in size and population. It is an archipelago consisting of around 150 relatively small islands, but with an impressive 137 million square kilometres of exclusive economic zone. Nearly 90% of the population resides on the largest island, Mahé, primarily in the capital Victoria. Victoria is approximately 1,300 kilometres from the coast of **Somalia** and about 1,000 kilometres from the northernmost point of **Madagascar.**

The archipelago is diverse in its origins – some islands are granitic, some are coral or raised coral islands, and there are also several coral sand keys and (for now) seven artificial islands or islands reclaimed from the sea. The majority of these islands are uninhabited, just as the entire archipelago was without a permanent inhabitant when it was discovered by Portuguese sailors under the command of Vasco da Gama in 1503. However, British sailors were the first to officially land a whole century later, in 1609. Britain and France competed for control over this small, strategically positioned archipelago. Seychelles was a British colony from 1810 until 1976, when the independent Republic of Seychelles was declared, and the country became a member of the Commonwealth.

A socialist one-party state was declared by the 1979 constitution, and the decade that followed was marked by numerous attempted coups. A multi-party system was only introduced in 1993, and today Seychelles ranks first in Africa in terms of electoral democracy, per capita GDP, Human Development Index, and as the country with the least corruption.

Seychelles is a blend of different cultures and peoples, originating from Europe, where the former colonial rulers were the French and the British; from **Africa**, which was the source of enslaved labour; and Asia, from where the Chinese and Indians – in particular, the Tamils – originate. The official languages are English, French, and Seychellois Creole. English is the language of business and law, but Creole is primarily used in parliament and everyday speech, supported by the state through the establishment of the Creole Institute and the adoption of an anthem in that language. Just as the main language of Seychelles is unique, so is the appearance of its flag, with its widening diagonal stripes radiating from the bottom left corner.

Until independence, plantations were of the greatest importance, but tourism is now the main source of income for the island nation with warm seas and beautiful beaches. Currently, the main agricultural products are sweet potatoes, coconuts, vanilla, and cinnamon, while the main export is fish.

The flora and fauna of Seychelles is extremely rich and diverse, with a large number of endemic species under the strict protection of the state. It has beauty large and small, with Moyenne Island, considered the world's smallest national park, covering an area of 10 hectares; and Aldabra Island, which is home to a large number of Aldabra giant tortoises, weighing up to 250 kilograms, and with the ability to reach leaves at a height of one metre using their long necks.

INTERNATIONAL ZONE OF
TANGIER

Tax-free haven in peace times

LOCATION: Northern Morocco
PERIOD: 1925–1956
AREA: 382 sq km
POPULATION: c. 185,000

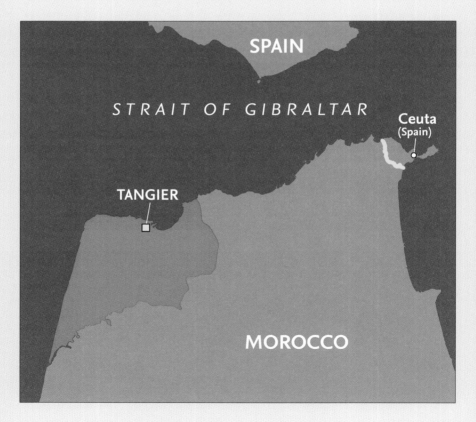

The Scramble for Africa was the process of conquering and dividing Africa among the European colonial powers in the second half of the 19th century, after which only **Liberia** and **Ethiopia** remained as independent countries. In the period before the beginning of the First World War, France and Spain completed the division of **Morocco**, with France obtaining the largest part of this African country, while Spain received the north (today's Mediterranean coast of Morocco) and the far south. The Sultan of Morocco retained only formal authority over his country. However, the strategic position of the city and port of Tangier (the birthplace of one of the greatest travellers of all time, Ibn Battuta) in the **Strait of Gibraltar**, at the entrance to the Mediterranean Sea, posed a stumbling block. The problem was resolved in 1923 by granting the city and its surrounding area the status of an International Zone based on a convention signed by Spain, France, and Great Britain, which insisted on the complete demilitarisation of the city. Over the next thirty years of the Zone's existence, the signatory countries frequently changed, among them the Netherlands, Sweden, Portugal, Italy, the US, and the USSR.

On 1 June 1925, Tangier officially became an International Zone, with the status of a tax haven with almost complete absence of any taxes. This lenient economic policy extended to other areas, making the Zone known for its large number of (non-transparent) banks and its cosmopolitan atmosphere and tolerance, which attracted numerous artists, intellectuals, businessmen, and spies. The executive authority over Tangier was held by an administrator appointed by the European powers, responsible for the entire territory and the European population; and by the Mendoub, the representative of the Sultan of Morocco, responsible for the Muslim and Jewish populations. The ethnic composition of the Zone consisted of approximately 50% Arabs and Berbers, 40% Europeans, and 10% Jews.

The German occupation of Paris at the beginning of the Second World War encouraged Spain to occupy Tangier as a measure of 'protection' against potential German or Italian occupation. The international governing bodies of Tangier were abolished, and the area was effectively annexed to Spanish Morocco. After the war, Spanish military forces withdrew, and the International Zone was restored, this time with the participation of representatives from the US and, temporarily, the USSR. When France and Spain granted independence to Morocco in 1956, changes also occurred in Tangier: the position of the European administrator was abolished, and instead, a Moroccan governor took over the leadership of the city-state. Just a few months later, on 29 October 1956, the participating powers returned Tangier to the sovereignty of Morocco, whose King Mohammed V granted the extension of tax privileges. However, in 1958, a major Berber rebellion erupted in the Rif region, a mountainous area along the Mediterranean coast of Morocco. This led to the abolition of the economic freedoms of the former Zone in 1960 and the end of Tangier's special status.

REPUBLIC OF **UTRECHT**

A Dutch microstate in the Zulu Kingdom

LOCATION: South Africa
PERIOD: mid-19th century
AREA: c. 2,000 sq km
POPULATION: c. 3,000

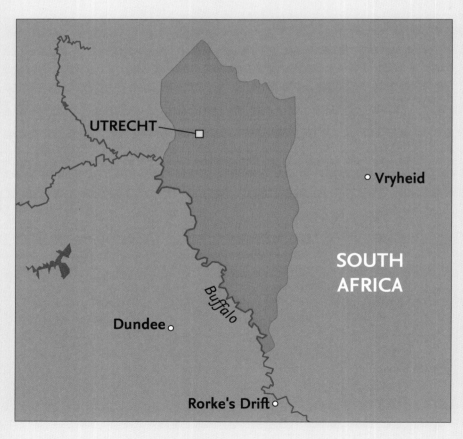

UTRECHT

° Vryheid

SOUTH AFRICA

Buffalo

Dundee °

Rorke's Drift °

0   30 km

Colonial conquests often led to the creation of huge colonial empires. A slightly rarer case was the creation of small, sometimes even isolated, colonies. The Republic of Utrecht was one such example. A brief review of the history of European colonisation of southern Africa will explain how and why this republic came into existence, and subsequently disappeared.

In the middle of the 17th century, the Kingdom of the **Netherlands** began the colonisation of **South Africa** by founding Cape Town and settling a large number of Dutch people in the surrounding areas. A century and a half later, the area became part of the British Empire, and the Dutch (also known as Boers, 'farmers', or *Voortrekkers*, 'pioneers') began the Great Trek, a great migration to the eastern and northeastern parts of present-day South Africa. This resulted in the establishment of several independent Boer republics, the most significant being the South African Republic (Transvaal), Orange Free State, and the Republic of Natalia. After only four years of existence, the Natalia was conquered by the British, who created the colony of Natal in 1843. Most of the Boers headed towards the remaining free Boer republics, but a few hundred decided to stay in the area not far from the Transvaal border, where they bought several hundred square kilometres of land between the Buffalo River and the Balele Mountains from the Zulu Kingdom (*KwaZul*). There, in the middle of the 19th century, they founded the town of Utrecht, named after the Dutch town from which many of them originated. The next step was a request for the accession of the town of Utrecht to the South African Republic, which was refused, so as not to provoke the British.

A few years later (in 1854) the residents of Utrecht decided to take matters into their own hands, forming the independent Republic of Utrecht. This Boer republic, approximately 30 by 60 kilometres in size, was home to several hundred Voortrekkers. It was one of the few Boer republics that chose the Dutch flag as its own. Despite having reasonably good relations with the neighbouring Zulu Kingdom (one of the Boer leaders was a personal friend of the Zulu King himself), the residents of Utrecht quickly realised that such a small area could hardly survive as an independent state. The same conclusion was reached by the inhabitants of another small Boer republic, the neighbouring Republic of Lydenburg, which led to the unification of these two in 1858. However, the change of borders continued: in 1860, the united Utrecht and Lydenburg joined the South African Republic. At the beginning of the 20th century, the British finally conquered the entire Transvaal, and transferred Utrecht to their Natal colony.

Today, the town of Utrecht has a population of about 35,000, and most of the inhabitants are engaged in mining and livestock farming. The town is located within a large wildlife reserve, so it is not unusual to see wild animals roaming freely in parks and gardens.

SULTANATE OF **ZANZIBAR**

Sultanate, republic, and birthplace of Queen

LOCATION: East coast of Africa
PERIOD: 1856–1964
AREA: 2,650 sq km
POPULATION: C. 300,000

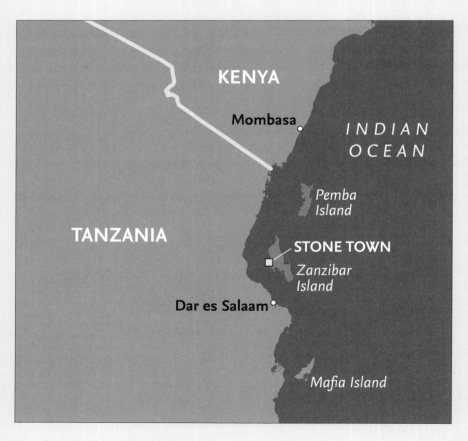

KENYA

Mombasa

INDIAN OCEAN

Pemba Island

TANZANIA

STONE TOWN

Zanzibar Island

Dar es Salaam

Mafia Island

0   200 km

The first half of the 19th century marked the peak of the expansion of the Sultanate of Oman, from the eastern regions of the Arabian Peninsula to vast areas along the east coast of Africa, and numerous islands in that part of the Indian Ocean. At the same time, Sultan Said bin Sultan decided to move his capital from ancient Muscat (now the capital of Oman) to the distant Stone Town on the island of **Zanzibar**. After his death in 1856, his two sons divided the inherited maritime power into two sultanates: Muscat and Oman in the north, and Zanzibar in the south.

Initially, the Sultanate of Zanzibar comprised the archipelago of the same name, including the largest islands of Zanzibar (Unguja) and Pemba, as well as the coast of present-day Kenya and Tanzania. Apart from the coastline, Zanzibar had significant influence over the local authorities of several vassal sultanates within the African interior. However, the continuous intrusion of British and German colonial forces began to reduce the Sultan's area of authority. This became particularly evident in 1890 when **Britain** and **Germany** signed a treaty, through which, among other things, Germany acquired what was known as German East Africa (the mainland part of present-day Tanzania), while the British gained rights over the then still independent Sultanate of Zanzibar. These rights immediately initiated the creation of a British protectorate, which lasted until 1963. Under pressure from Germany, Zanzibar renounced the coastal strip of present-day Tanzania, while the Sultan retained only formal authority over the Protectorate of Kenya, a narrow coastal strip of present-day **Kenya**. The rest of the country was an official British colony at the time, although the aforementioned strip was effectively part of this colony.

In 1963, major changes occurred in this part of Africa: on 10 December, Great Britain terminated its protectorate over Zanzibar; the Sultan of the now-independent Zanzibar immediately, in agreement with the British, renounced rights to the coastal strip of Kenya; the Colony of Kenya gained independence and united with the former Protectorate of Kenya to form the independent state of Kenya. However, the Sultan of Zanzibar had little time to rejoice, as only one month later, he was overthrown from power by his African subjects, and the monarchy was replaced by the new socialist People's Republic of Zanzibar on 12 January 1964. The creation of this state was accompanied by bloody violence.

However, even socialist Zanzibar did not last long as a state, as it united with Tanganyika at the end of April, to form the United Republic of Tanganyika and Zanzibar, which a few months later became the United Republic of Tanzania (a completely new name, formed by combining the names TANganyika and ZANzibar). Today, Zanzibar has a semi-autonomous status within Tanzania.

In Stone Town, or Mji Mkongwe ('old town' in Swahili), the capital of the Sultanate of Zanzibar, on 5 September 1946, Farrokh Bulsara was born into a Zoroastrian (Parsi) family of Western Indian origin. In **London**, in 1970, he founded the rock band Queen along with Brian May, Roger Taylor and John Deacon, and officially changed his name to Freddie Mercury.

AMERICAS

Established in 1765, the St Vincent and the Grenadines Botanic Gardens played an important role in the islands' agricultural development.

REPUBLIC OF **ANGUILLA**

Microstate that drove out overseas authority

LOCATION: Caribbean region
PERIOD: 1967–1969
AREA: 91 sq km
POPULATION: c. 6,000

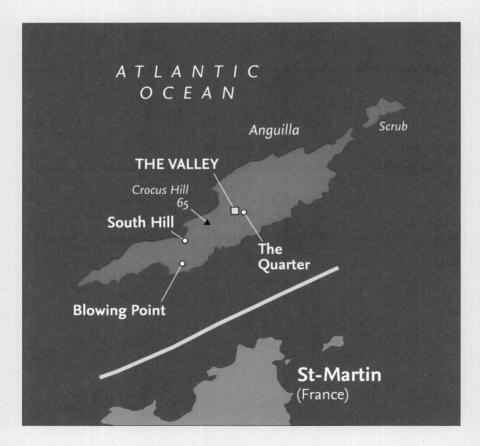

ATLANTIC OCEAN

Anguilla

Scrub

THE VALLEY

Crocus Hill
65

South Hill

The Quarter

Blowing Point

St-Martin
(France)

0   5 km

During its colonial rule, **Britain** had numerous Caribbean islands under its control and, occasionally, decisions were made to group some of these islands together, into one larger colony, to facilitate easier and more efficient management of these distant parts of the Empire. An example of this was uniting the islands of **Anguilla** and **Nevis** under the governance of the larger island of **St Kitts** in the mid-19th century, with the new name: St Kitts-Nevis-Anguilla. This led to frequent protests on both forcibly annexed islands, but without significant results. After the Second World War, St Kitts-Nevis-Anguilla was part of the West Indies Federation from 1958 to 1962, and in 1967 it gained the status of an associated state with wide autonomy from Britain. However, the residents of Anguilla (and Nevis) felt neglected by the government of this joint state, which they primarily viewed as the government of St Kitts.

The formation of the associated state marked the beginning of constant protests and violence on Anguilla. In late May 1967, mass gatherings of protestors resulted in the complete expulsion of the police force from the island (the police force comprising only 15 or so officers from St Kitts). The next day, a committee of prominent Anguillan residents was formed, whose main tasks were to preserve normality and to separate from St Kitts. A few weeks later, a referendum was held asking the residents of Anguilla if they wanted to secede from St Kitts. The answer was definitive: 99% of Anguillans voted in favour of secession, and so the independence of the island was immediately declared and a constitution adopted. A new flag was also introduced, featuring three orange dolphins, which remains the basis of Anguilla's coat of arms and flag to this day.

Negotiations between Anguilla, St Kitts, and Britain, with the assistance of other Caribbean members of the **Commonwealth**, lasted until the end of 1967. The result was the separation of Anguilla from the joint state and the acceptance of some form of temporary direct control by Britain. At the beginning of 1969, a referendum was held again, reaffirming the islanders' desire for independence and leading to the immediate declaration of the independent Republic of Anguilla. A British representative proposed a new British administration over the island, but was driven from the island by force.

This time, the British were unwilling to wait any longer, so on 19 March 1969, nearly 400 soldiers and police landed on Anguilla to 'restore peace'. The miniature republic was thus abolished, but the main wish of the Anguillans was achieved: their island became a separate British Crown colony, with no political ties to St Kitts.

Today, Anguilla is a prosperous and politically stable United Kingdom Overseas Territory, enjoying internal self-governance. It also shares the same currency: the East Caribbean dollar. Apart from the two United Kingdom Overseas Territories (Anguilla and **Montserrat**), this dollar is the official currency in six sovereign states (**Antigua and Barbuda**, **Dominica**, **Grenada**, St Kitts and Nevis, **St Lucia**, and **St Vincent and the Grenadines**), some of which will be discussed in the following pages of this book.

ANTIGUA AND BARBUDA

Wadadli and Wa'omoni

LOCATION: Caribbean region
PERIOD: since 1981
AREA: 442 sq km
POPULATION: 93,763

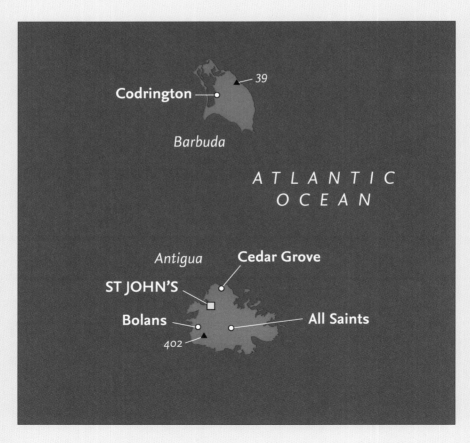

The Lesser Antilles are a chain of small islands between **Puerto Rico** and South America, and form the boundary between the Caribbean Sea and the Atlantic Ocean. This chain consists of eight sovereign states and a large number of dependent territories, which belong to the **United Kingdom**, **France**, the **Netherlands**, and the **United States**. The northernmost of these independent states is Antigua and Barbuda.

Although tropical, Antigua and Barbuda is a very dry island country, consisting of two main islands, Antigua and Barbuda, and several smaller islands. The capital, St John's, is located on the island of Antigua, and is home to approximately 97% of the country's population. Most of the present-day population traces its origins to West Africa, with significantly smaller numbers from Britain, **Portugal**, and East Asia. English is the official language, although it is not stated in the constitution.

From a European perspective, Christopher Columbus discovered these islands in 1493. They were already inhabited by the Taino and Kalinago (previously known as Carib, a term that is now considered offensive) peoples, after which the Caribbean islands and the Caribbean Sea were named. Columbus named the island of Antigua after a Spanish church, although the local people still refer to it by its old name, Wadadli; Barbuda was originally Wa'omoni. European colonisation of the islands began in 1632 when the British occupied Antigua, followed by Barbuda in 1678. At that time, cultivation of sugar cane and tobacco began, using enslaved labour from Africa. Enslavement was abolished in the first half of the 19th century.

The first step towards independence for Antigua and Barbuda came in 1958 when it became part of the West Indies Federation. This federation of British Caribbean colonies had broad internal self-government, with the eventual goal of gaining independence from Britain, much like Canada and Australia. Unfortunately, numerous internal conflicts led to the dissolution of the Federation in 1962, and in 1981, Antigua and Barbuda finally became an independent state, with the British monarch as the formal head. Proposals for holding a referendum on a republican form of government for the small Caribbean state are becoming increasingly frequent.

The economy of Antigua and Barbuda is primarily based on tourism and financial services. Both main islands are relatively flat and low, with the highest elevation at 402 metres above sea level. The irregularly shaped coastlines are full of bays and beaches, which attract tourists, especially when combined with the vibrant culture and rich historical heritage. Life is expensive on the islands, with agriculture failing to meet domestic needs, mainly due to a lack of water and skilled labour.

Destructive hurricanes are relatively common. In 2017, Hurricane Irma forced most of Barbuda's residents to find temporary shelter on Antigua after destroying many of its buildings. Barbuda's population of 1,500 is concentrated in Codrington, the island's only town, however, even with such a small population, there are frequent clarion calls for the creation of a dual federation or even for the full independence of Barbuda.

Named after King James II of England, Fort James was
built in the early 18th century to guard the entrance to
the harbour of St John's, Antigua and Barbuda.

Gun Hill Signal Station in Barbados was one of a network of signal stations built in 1818 to sight ships approaching the island.

BARBADOS

Sugar, rum, and democratic governance

LOCATION: Caribbean region
PERIOD: since 1966
AREA: 430 sq km
POPULATION: 281,635

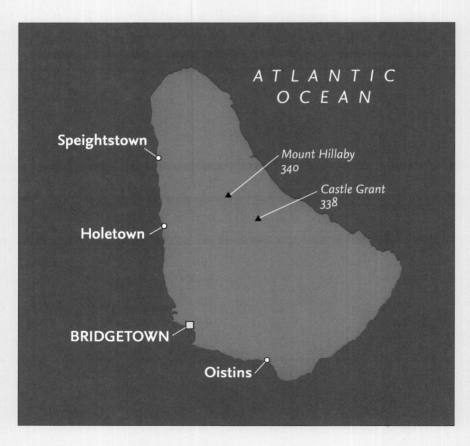

ATLANTIC OCEAN

Speightstown

Mount Hillaby
340

Castle Grant
338

Holetown

BRIDGETOWN

Oistins

0   5 km

The first inhabitants of the island of Barbados were members of South American Taino tribes, who settled at the beginning of the 9th century, and Kalinago tribes, who arrived on the island in the 13th century. The oldest recorded name for Barbados was Ichirouganaim. In the 16th century, the Spanish occasionally visited the island, primarily to kidnap the local people for enslaved labour on their plantations. However, the first European settlements were established by the English in the first half of the 17th century, and the island officially became an English (later, British) colony in 1663. It retained this status until the mid-20th century.

For the requirements of the plantations in Barbados, British ships brought a large number of enslaved people from Africa, which is why today about 90% of the island's population is of African descent. At the same time, indentured workers were forcibly brought from **Ireland**; their descendants were known as 'poor Whites' (or 'Redlegs'). However, this community has almost completely disappeared today.

During the centuries of British rule over Barbados, sugar cultivation on large plantations was the main source of income. Poor living and working conditions led to rebellions by the enslaved people and other poor populations, demanding freedom, and better economic conditions. Similar to other neighbouring small island nations in the Caribbean, the path to independence began with the **West Indies Federation**, a union of several British colonies aiming for joint independence. This federation existed from 1958 to 1962, when it collapsed due to numerous internal conflicts. Over the next four years, Barbados was a self-governing colony, and in 1966 it became an independent constitutional monarchy. The British Queen Elizabeth II was the head of the state, serving as the Queen of Barbados, a role she held until the declaration of the Republic on 30 November 2021. In the early 1990s, there were proposals for the creation of a federation between Barbados, **Guyana**, and **Trinidad and Tobago**, but the project was quickly forgotten.

Barbados can be proud of its democratic governance throughout all its years of independence, which has provided a favourable foundation for a stable society and a strong economy. Historically, the economy relied on sugar production, while in modern times, tourism, financial services, the IT sector, and the oil industry have taken precedence. Perhaps the most famous 'export' of this small tropical island is the international pop star Rihanna, who has gained numerous musical awards and is one of the best-selling artists worldwide.

Barbados is believed to have been the only place outside the **United States** that George Washington visited. The house where he allegedly stayed as a young man is now under the protection of UNESCO, although some historians contest that this is the correct house.

Barbados is often claimed to be the birthplace of rum, which remains a significant product to this day, and fried or steamed flying fish is one of the specialties of the island cuisine.

CANUDOS

From beautiful hill to bloodstained lake

LOCATION: Eastern Brazil
PERIOD: 1893–1897
AREA: a few hundred square kilometres
POPULATION: C. 30,000

When Isabel, Princess Imperial of **Brazil**, signed the so-called 'Golden Law' in 1888, abolishing enslavement in her country (only one year before the overthrow of the monarchy and the proclamation of the First Brazilian Republic), she may not have foreseen what was to come for Brazil. The law declared enslavement illegal, but provided no reparations, land or mechanisms to enable the formerly enslaved people to integrate with Brazilian society. This resulted in millions of men, women and children becoming homeless. A large number of poor peasants and formerly enslaved people were attracted by the sermons of preachers and travelling priests, among whom Antônio Conselheiro ('Antônio the Counsellor') stood out.

The new republican authorities were not too thrilled with Conselheiro's pro-monarchist views, so in 1893, he set out for the *sertão*, a sparsely populated and arid region in northeastern Brazil, with a number of his followers, who were known as *conselheiristas*. On an abandoned farm, they founded a settlement which Conselheiro named Belo Monte ('Beautiful Hill'), but which later became better known as Canudos because of the abundance of the canudo-de-pita plant.

Antônio Conselheiro was regarded as a messiah and saint, who imposed strict religious rules on his village. Canudos became a sort of utopia, where the poor inhabitants were given plots of land to produce food for themselves; the entire village raised communal herds of cattle; the currency and laws of Brazil were rejected and ignored; and all residents participated in decision-making.

In just a few years, word of Canudos spread throughout Brazil, and many flocked there, with the population soon reaching nearly 30,000 people. This meant fewer workers on the large farms across the surrounding Brazilian province of **Bahia**, and so wealthy landowners demanded that the 'microstate' of Canudos be crushed militarily, arguing that it was a monarchist rebellion. A military intervention was attempted, but, unexpectedly, the first three attacks by the Brazilian army were repelled in bloody battles with the inhabitants of the town. However, the fourth attack, under the command of as many as five generals and the Minister of Defence, lasted from June to October of 1897. 'Beautiful Hill' was attacked by about 12,000 heavily armed soldiers and police, of which almost 5,000 died. On the other side, almost all of the 25,000 conselheiristas were killed (Conselheiro himself died in September 1897), and the town was practically levelled to the ground. Several decades later the Cocorobó Dam was built there, and its artificial lake has flooded the ruined capital of the former promised land. **Canudos State Park** was created in 1986 not far away, as a kind of open-air museum dedicated to the massacre in the War of Canudos.

During this bloody conflict, a large group of soldiers was stationed on the nearby hill of Morro de Favela (*favela* is the name of an endemic plant in that region). After the fighting ended, the Brazilian government allowed them to settle on the Morro da Providência (Providencia Hill) in **Rio da Janeiro** - thus creating Brazil's first residential *favela* ('shantytown').

COMMONWEALTH OF
DOMINICA

The nature island of the Caribbean

LOCATION: Caribbean region
PERIOD: since 1978
AREA: 750 sq km
POPULATION: 72,737

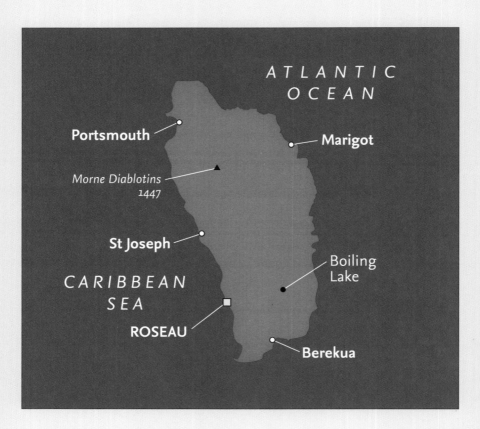

ATLANTIC OCEAN

Portsmouth

Marigot

Morne Diablotins
1447

St Joseph

Boiling Lake

CARIBBEAN SEA

ROSEAU

Berekua

0   10 km

The Caribbean islands and the sea with the same name, take their name from the Kalinago people (previously known as Carib people, a term that is now considered offensive) who inhabited numerous islands between North and South America. European colonisation of the region led to the almost complete extermination of this people. The majority of the remaining 3,000 members of the Kalinago people inhabit the Kalinago Territory, a 15-square-kilometre area in the east of Dominica, a small island country in the middle of the **Lesser Antilles**. Although the language has practically died out, along with the original name of the island, Waitukubuli, customs are alive under the protection of local authorities, led by a chief and council.

European colonisers – first the French, and then the British – encountered considerable difficulties in conquering the mountainous regions of Dominica, where Kalinago warriors fiercely resisted for almost 200 years. However, this did not prevent them establishing plantations on the island and bringing a large number of enslaved African people, and in 1763, the island officially became a British colony. An independent republic was proclaimed in 1978.

Dominica is considered one of the poorer countries of the **Eastern Caribbean**, and a significant source of income comes from the cultivation of bananas, coffee, and mangoes. The relatively small number of beaches has hindered rapid development of tourism, but ecotourism has flourished due to the mountains (the highest peak is 1,447 metres), dense rainforests, waterfalls, lakes, and hot springs. Dominica is home to the Boiling Lake, the second-largest hot spring in the world after Frying Pan Lake in **New Zealand**. Boiling Lake varies in size and depth, with water temperatures reaching 90 °C along the shores, and significantly higher in the middle. The mystical effect of the lake and surrounding dense vegetation is enhanced by the large amount of steam that evaporates and surrounds this natural wonder. The beautiful Boeri Lake is nearby, located in a volcanic crater at an altitude of more than 800 metres above sea level. The sea around Dominica is known as an excellent location for another tourist attraction: whale watching. Thus, it is not surprising that Dominica has earned the title 'The Nature Island of the Caribbean' among nature lovers.

Today, the majority of the population of Dominica are of African descent, with a small minority of European origin. The official language is English, but Dominican Creole, based on the French language, is also used, which is a result of first French and then British rule. Sylvanie Burton became Dominica's first female president when she was elected in 2023, and was the first member of the Kalinago indigenous population to lead this small Caribbean state.

The Sisserou parrot, also known as the imperial amazon, is an endemic and highly endangered species of parrot with purple feathers. It has been estimated there are only about fifty of them remaining today. This bird inhabits the mountainous region of Dominica, but it also appears on the country's flag, one of the few national flags that have the colour purple on it.

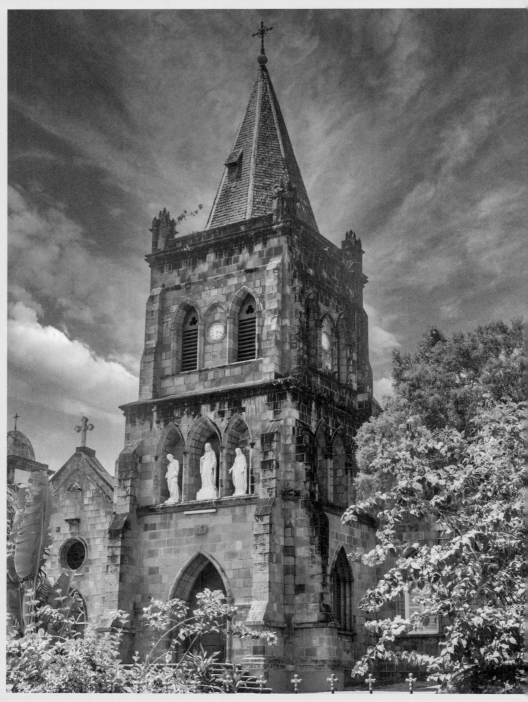

Cathedral of Our Lady of Fair Haven, in the Dominican capital of Roseau, is built from volcanic stone and has been designed to withstand earthquakes.

A vintage car contributes to the colourful scene on Old Street in Philipsburg, the capital of Sint Maarten, Kingdom of the Netherlands.

DUTCH CARIBBEAN

The BES and CAS islands

LOCATION: Caribbean region
PERIOD: since 2010

ARUBA
AREA: 193 sq km
POPULATION: 106,445

CURAÇAO
AREA: 444 sq km
POPULATION: 191,163

SINT MAARTEN
AREA: 34 sq km
POPULATION: 44,175

CARIBBEAN SEA

Anguilla

St-Martin

Sint Maarten
PHILIPSBURG

St-Barthélemy

Saba
(Neth.)

St Eustatius
(Neth.)

ST KITTS AND NEVIS

Aruba

CARIBBEAN SEA

Curaçao

ORANJESTAD

Bonaire
(Neth.)

WILLEMSTAD

VENEZUELA

0   30 km

For centuries, the Caribbean islands were under the rule of European colonial powers, including the **Netherlands**. Over time, the local populations achieved several independent states, and the remaining colonies also gained increasingly broader self-government. The Dutch colonies were given broad autonomy in 1954 when two constituent states were formed within the Kingdom of the Netherlands: **Suriname** (in northern South America) and the Netherlands Antilles. The third constituent state of this country was the Netherlands proper in Europe. The Netherlands Antilles consisted of several former Dutch island colonies. **Aruba**, **Curaçao**, and **Bonaire** are located south of the Caribbean Sea, along the coast of **Venezuela**; while **Sint Maarten**, **St Eustatius**, and **Saba** are situated to the east of **Puerto Rico**. On the southern islands, the majority of the population speaks Papiamento, a language that originated from a mixture of Portuguese, Spanish, Dutch, West African, and native languages, while the northern islands are predominantly English-speaking.

The Netherlands Antilles had never felt stable, and Aruba was the first to secede in 1986, while the other islands remained under the common flag until 2010. An agreement was reached then between all the islands and the Dutch government, according to which the Netherlands Antilles was dissolved, and out of the six former member islands, three special municipalities (Bonaire, St Eustatius, and Saba – the BES islands) were formed within the Netherlands proper, and three self-governing states (Curaçao, Aruba, and Sint Maarten – the CAS islands) were established within the Kingdom of the Netherlands. Officially, these three Caribbean countries within the Kingdom of the Netherlands have the same status and position as the 'European' Netherlands (with its three municipalities (BES islands) in the Caribbean), even though they only make up 5% of the land area and population of the Kingdom of the Netherlands.

The Kingdom of the Netherlands is in charge of foreign policy and defence, but other areas of governance are largely under the control of the local parliaments of the CAS islands and their governments. Each of the CAS islands sends its Minister Plenipotentiary to the Netherlands, where they, together with ministers of the Dutch government, form the Council of Ministers of the Kingdom, but also represent the interests of their islands in the Netherlands and Europe.

Although there are similarities among the CAS islands, there are some noticeable differences too. The official languages in Aruba are Dutch and Papiamento; in Curaçao, it's Dutch, Papiamento, and English; while in Sint Maarten, Dutch and English are used. Sint Maarten is the only state with a land border – with the French community of St-Martin which occupies the northern half of the island of St-Martin. The official currency in Aruba is the Aruban florin, while the remaining two CAS islands use the Netherlands Antillean guilder. The US dollar can also be used in most shops on the CAS islands.

The somewhat confusing political status of the Dutch Caribbean islands doesn't stop them from being popular tourist destinations, known for breathtaking beaches and crystal-clear water, as well as cuisine, music, and dances – blending a perfect mix of European, African, and indigenous influences.

GRENADA

Spice island

LOCATION: Caribbean region
PERIOD: since 1974
AREA: 378 sq km
POPULATION: 125,438

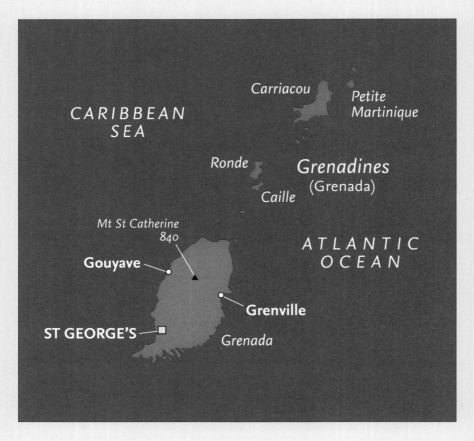

Grenada is the southernmost island in the Windward Islands group, located approximately 140 kilometres north of **Venezuela** and **Trinidad**. The island, originally named Camerhougue by the indigenous Kalinago people, was 'discovered' by Christopher Columbus in 1498. It is presumed that the dense forest reminded the Spanish sailors of the surroundings of Granada, the famous city in Andalusia, which is why they gave the island its current name. From the mid-17th to the late 18th century, Grenada was a French colony, during which cocoa and sugar cane cultivation began using enslaved labour from Africa. **Britain** became the new colonial power in 1763. The intense development of island plantations created the need for bringing more and more enslaved people. The cultivation of nutmeg began during British rule on the island, and eventually became one the most significant products of Grenada – which is still the world's second-largest producer of this spice today – and it proudly features on the country's flag.

From 1958 to 1962, Grenada was part of the **West Indies Federation**, a union of British Caribbean colonies. After the federation dissolved, Grenada gained broad internal autonomy, and in 1974 it became an independent state, with the British monarch at the head. Just five years later, a coup was launched, bringing communists to power on the island, although somewhat paradoxically, Queen Elizabeth II remained sovereign. In terms of foreign policy, the communist government made alliances with **Cuba**, **Nicaragua**, and other countries with a similar political orientation. At the end of 1983, conflicts broke out within the government of Grenada when the prime minister was killed under unclear circumstances. This event prompted the Governor-General of Grenada, as a representative of the British crown, to request that the **United States** and neighbouring Caribbean states conduct a military intervention to restore order in the country. Several thousand US soldiers arrived, and within a few days of a successful intervention, they began withdrawing to their bases. Grenada has since been a politically stable state with a democratic system of government.

The official language of Grenada is English, but the majority of the population uses Grenadian Creole English on a daily basis, while Patwa LaGwinad (Grenadian Creole French) is spoken by around 2,000 residents in rural areas. Approximately four-fifths of the population is of African descent.

In addition to the island of Grenada itself, the southern part of the Grenadines archipelago, and the islands of **Carriacou** and **Petite Martinique**, are also a part of the state of Grenada, and the constitution provides for local autonomy for these (the first steps toward establishing this internal self-government have been initiated). Tourism is an extremely significant source of income, so it is no surprise to find tourist hotspots like the Carriacou Regatta, chocolate festivals, or Spicemas, a colourful carnival enriched with the melodies of soca and calypso music. North of the capital, St George's, lies the Molinere Bay Underwater Sculpture Park, where divers can enjoy fantastic and eerie sculptures submerged in the shallow waters.

Since the first sculptures were installed in 2006, the Molinere Bay Underwater Sculpture Park has relieved pressure from tourism on the coral reefs off the west coast of Grenada.

This metal stele commemorating Luther Parker, justice of the peace for the Republic of Indian Stream, is located in the town park of Pittsburg, New Hampshire.

REPUBLIC OF
INDIAN STREAM

*Double taxation
on a disputed river*

LOCATION: New Hampshire, United States
PERIOD: 1832–1835
AREA: c. 700 sq km
POPULATION: C. 400

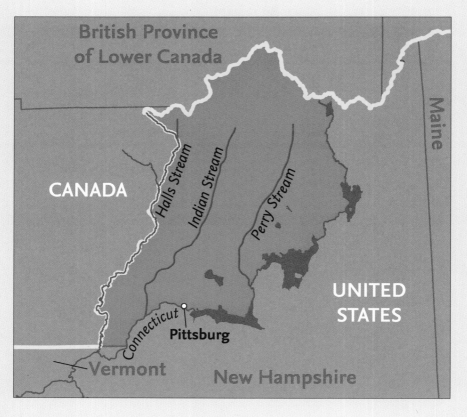

0   10 km

The great conflict between **Britain** and the rebellious American colonies ended with the signing of the Treaty of Paris in 1783. Apart from ending the conflict, this peace agreement also led to the independence of the 'ancestor' of the **United States**, in the area west of the Mississippi River and south of the Great Lakes. The borders between the areas which would later become the US and **Canada** (at that time still part of the British Empire) were defined as best they could be in those days without GPS, flights and satellites, and naturally there were areas up for debate.

One such questionable case was near the Connecticut River, New England's longest river. The peace treaty emphasised that the American–British border there ran along one of the tributaries of this river, but it was not clear on which one. Both the British and the Americans believed that it was the one that gave them more territory, so they each started sending their tax collectors to the area around the Indian Stream River. The inhabitants certainly were not thrilled with this double taxation, so all 400 of them complained to the then British colony of Lower Canada and the United States, but received no concrete answer.

The behaviour of their large neighbours led to a gathering of the inhabitants, who declared the area independent under the name of Republic of Indian Stream (RIS) in 1832. A constitution was also adopted, which was democratic for that time. The government of the newly proclaimed state consisted of an Assembly (of which every adult resident could be a member) and a Council of five members. A militia of about 40 members was established, which was commanded by the government. Although the state seemed to function well, everyone was aware that an area with such a small population could hardly survive as an independent territory. Therefore the constitution emphasised that independence was declared to allow the area to function normally until it was made clear to which government (American or British/Canadian) it actually belonged.

The existence of this new neighbour was largely ignored by both American and British authorities (although for some time the American authorities levied customs duties on goods imported from the Republic of Indian Stream, just as if they were from abroad), until an occasion in 1835 when an American sheriff requested the assistance of the military due to some problems in Indian Stream. When the army reached the border, the sheriff visited the Assembly, where he issued an ultimatum. Realising that the Americans were serious, the Assembly decided to disband the RIS and annex the Republic to the state of New Hampshire. The border between the US and Canada in this region was only officially agreed upon in 1842, allowing for another microstate to appear just 350 kilometres from Indian Stream, in 1827 – the Republic of Madawaska, which lasted only a few months.

Today, the area of the Republic of Indian Stream largely coincides with the territory of the city of Pittsburg, New Hampshire, where several historical markers record the existence of this almost forgotten microstate.

FEDERATION OF
ST KITTS AND NEVIS

Fertile lands of peaks and rivers

LOCATION: Caribbean region
PERIOD: since 1983
AREA: 261 sq km
POPULATION: 47,657

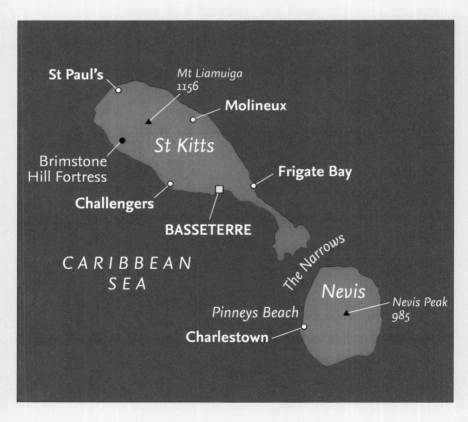

St Paul's

Mt Liamuiga
1156

Molineux

St Kitts

Brimstone
Hill Fortress

Frigate Bay

Challengers

BASSETERRE

*CARIBBEAN
SEA*

The Narrows

Nevis

Nevis Peak
985

Pinneys Beach

Charlestown

0   10 km

The smallest independent state in the Americas, and the smallest federation in the world, is St Kitts and Nevis, a tiny country located 300 kilometres east of **Puerto Rico**. It consists of two islands, the larger St Kitts and the smaller Nevis, separated by a strait called The Narrows, which is only 3 kilometres wide. A dense rainforest covers mostly uninhabited central mountainous areas of both islands, with the highest peaks reaching 1,156 metres on St Kitts and 985 metres on Nevis. Both islands have numerous rivers and streams which originate in the mountainous regions and provide irrigation to the fertile land on the coastal plains.

According to historical sources, Christopher Columbus arrived at the islands in 1493, and supposedly named them San Cristóbal and San Martín. The English translated the name of the first island as St Christopher's Island, which eventually became St Kitts. Today, it is officially permitted to use both the older, longer form of the name and the newer, shorter form. The name of the island San Martín was changed to Nuestra Señora de las Nieves ('Our Lady of the Snows'), from which the current form Nevis is derived. Both islands had their Kalinago names centuries before the arrival of Europeans: the larger one was called Liamuiga ('fertile land'), and the smaller one was Oualie ('island of beautiful waters').

The first European settlers were the English, whose settlement from 1623 is considered the oldest European colony in the Caribbean. Soon after, the French also arrived, and together with the English, they divided the island. Following the massacre of the local Kalinago people in 1626, the English and French brought a large number of enslaved people from West Africa to work for them. Consequentially, 90% of the federation's population is of African descent. The official language on both islands is English, but in everyday communication, the majority of the population uses St Kitts Creole, or Nevis Creole or Nevisian, in Nevis.

St Kitts and Nevis was part of the **West Indies Federation** from 1958 to 1962, and gained full independence in 1983, with the British monarch as the formal head of state. According to the agreement, Nevis has the right to hold a referendum where citizens would vote on whether they wanted independence. This right was exercised in 1998 when 62% of Nevisians voted for independence for their island. However, the constitution requires a minimum of two-thirds of voters to vote in favour, so Nevis remained within the federation, albeit with relatively broad autonomy and its own prime minister and parliament.

Tourism is certainly a driving force on both islands, contributed to by numerous festivals, the exceptionally preserved Brimstone Hill Fortress, lush nature, the St Kitts Scenic Railway, and the five-kilometre-long Pinneys Beach on the west coast of Nevis. In Charlestown, the capital of Nevis, there is a two-storey house, where the ground floor functions as the Museum of Nevis History, while the first floor is reserved for the Nevis Island Assembly. Although historically unconfirmed, it is said that Alexander Hamilton (one of the Founding Fathers, the first Secretary of the Treasury of the **United States** and leader of the ruling Federalist Party) was born in that house.

ST LUCIA

An island fought over for more than 1,800 years

LOCATION: Caribbean region
PERIOD: since 1979
AREA: 616 sq km
POPULATION: 179,857

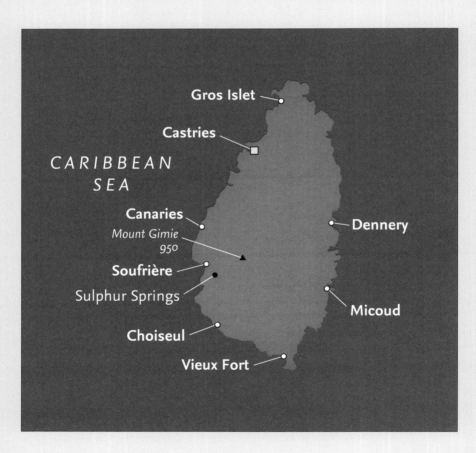

Gros Islet

Castries

CARIBBEAN SEA

Canaries

Mount Gimie
950

Dennery

Soufrière

Sulphur Springs

Micoud

Choiseul

Vieux Fort

0   10 km

There are volcanoes all over the world, but only one bears the title of 'The World's Only Drive-In Volcano' – Sulphur Springs on the Caribbean Island of St Lucia. This UNESCO World Heritage Site constitutes a large geothermal field, situated within the crater of an ancient volcano between Gros and Petit Piton, two impressive volcanic plugs. A road passes in close vicinity, allowing tourists to enjoy the sight of powerful jets of steam, producing incredible visual effects against an already movie-style backdrop. Nearby, people can bathe in warm sulphur mud which is believed to have medicinal properties.

St Lucia is a small island in the **Lesser Antilles**, located about 350 kilometres north of Venezuela and Trinidad. The Taino people settled on the island in the 3rd century, naming it Iouanalao, but the Kalinago people renamed it Hewanorra, after defeating the Tainos in the 9th century. In the mid-17th century, the French established the first European settlements, and the island was later named after St Lucy of Syracuse, a female saint from the end of the 3rd and early 4th centuries. This makes St Lucia the only sovereign state named after a woman (although there is not enough evidence to conclusively prove that Lucy definitely existed). Soon after the French, the English arrived on the island, which caused numerous conflicts between the two powers over the next nearly 150 years.

Finally, in 1814, after the defeat of Napoleon Bonaparte, St Lucia officially became a British colony. During the Second World War, German U-boats sank two British ships in **Castries**, the capital and main harbour of St Lucia. After the war, St Lucia became a member of the **West Indies Federation** from 1958 to 1962, and gained independence in 1979, retaining the British monarch as the formal head of state.

The production and export of bananas brings significant revenue to this small island country, and has led to improved infrastructure and overall quality of life. Towards the end of the 20th and beginning of the 21st century, tourism became more and more important, but banana, mango, coconut, and avocado cultivation still contribute to the national economy. There is also growing development in the production of electronics, cardboard, and clothing.

St Lucia is an island of volcanic origin, with high forested mountains in the interior (the highest peak is 950 metres), where numerous rivers source, bringing life to fertile plains along the coast. These plains are the most densely populated areas, and the majority of the population – over 85% – is descended from enslaved Africans. The official language is English, but the long French rule influenced the St Lucian Creole language (also known as Kwéyòl or patwa), based on French vocabulary with the syntax of African languages. The media and government use this Creole language to a great extent, and there are often requests for it to become the second official language in Sent Lisi, as St Lucia is called in Kwéyòl.

ST VINCENT AND THE GRENADINES

Land of bananas and tiny islands

LOCATION: Caribbean region
PERIOD: since 1979
AREA: 389 sq km
POPULATION: 103,948

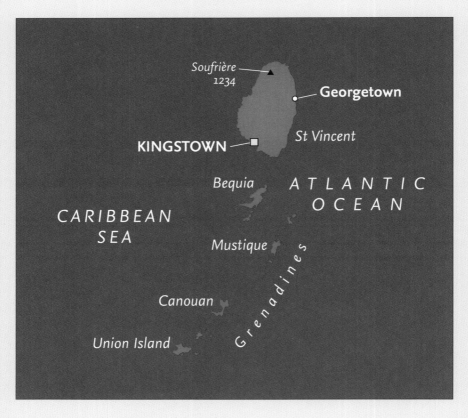

Soufrière
1234

Georgetown

St Vincent

KINGSTOWN

Bequia

ATLANTIC
OCEAN

CARIBBEAN
SEA

Mustique

Canouan

Grenadines

Union Island

0   25 km

St Vincent and the Grenadines (SVG) is a small Caribbean country that is part of the island chain of the **Lesser Antilles**. It consists of the large island of St Vincent and around 30 islands that form part of the Grenadines island chain (the southern third of which belongs to Grenada). At least ten of the islands are inhabited.

The island of St Vincent is of volcanic origin, predominantly mountainous and rich in dense forests. The highest peak is the volcano **Soufrière**, at 1,234 metres. The volcanic soil is very fertile, which is why bananas, the main domestic product, thrive here, though tourism has now taken that sweet, top income spot. The Grenadines are increasingly emerging as a significant tourist centre, helped undoubtedly by the construction of several airports on the islands, making them more accessible to tourists from all over the world.

Similar to many other Caribbean islands, the population of SVG is mainly of African descent (around 70%), while the population of European origin mostly descends from the Portuguese. English is used in all official domains, but almost the entire population predominately speaks Vincentian Creole, a blend of English, Spanish, Kalinago, and various African languages, in everyday life.

Like other Caribbean islands, a similar story unfolds about St Vincent's name. When Columbus reached the islands and brought it to the attention of the Europeans, it was inhabited by the Kalinago people, who called it Youloumain, after *Youlouca*, the spirit of the rainbow. Despite fierce resistance from the indigenous Kalinago people, the French occupied part of the island, where they established their first plantations of sugar cane, coffee, tobacco, and cocoa. They brought a large number of enslaved African people to work on the plantations. People of mixed African and Kalinago or Taino descent, are called Garifuna people here. They started two wars with the British, who had taken over the island from the French in the meantime. The superior British army eventually triumphed over the Garifuna after four years, punishing them with mass deportation to the island of Roatán, Honduras, and Baliceaux, in the Grenadines. Those who went to Baliceaux faced an island with no fresh water or food, and more than half of them died within a short time. The survivors joined their compatriots in Honduras, where there are several hundred thousand of them today. On the other hand, it is estimated that there are only several dozen of these peoples still in SVG.

Together with its neighbours, SVG became part of the **West Indies Federation**, a union of former British colonies, in 1958. The federation dissolved in 1962, and SVG gained independence in 1979. Exactly 30 years later, a referendum was held, in which the citizens rejected the idea of their country becoming a republic.

ASIA

The 8.6-metre-tall statue in Singapore's Merlion Park has the body of a fish and the head of a lion, representing the city's origin as a fishing village, and its name, which is based on the Sanskrit for 'City of Lions'.

AHI REPUBLIC

A brotherhood of craftsmen

LOCATION: present-day Turkey
PERIOD: c. 1290–1362
AREA: 100–300 sq km
POPULATION: unknown

The Byzantine defeat at the Battle of Manzikert in 1071 marked the gradual retreat of the weakened **Eastern Roman Empire** from Asia Minor (Anatolia) and the invasion of the Turkish-Persian Great Seljuk Empire. Just six years later, Seljuk territories in Anatolia separated and formed a new state, the Sultanate of Rûm (Rûm was the common Turkish name for the Roman state and people). However, the Mongol invasion and the defeat at the Battle of Köse Dağ in 1243 marked the end of the independent sultanate, which became a vassal of the Mongol Empire (and its successor, the Ilkhanate) for the next 60 years. The weakening authority of the sultans led to the gradual decline of the Seljuk state and the formation of a large number of semi-independent Anatolian beyliks (principalities or duchies). The most powerful among them, the Ottoman Beylik, slowly united all Turkish states, eventually growing into the **Ottoman Empire**, one of the greatest world powers of all time. However, numerous small beyliks, like the Ahi Republic, lasted much longer and contributed to the creation of the future Turkish state.

The Ahi Republic, previously known as the Ahi Brotherhood, initially represented a kind of craftsman's guild that was widespread throughout the Sultanate of Rûm. The guild was founded by the preacher, philosopher, and poet Ahi Evran, also known as Pir Ahi Evran-ı Veli. He was born in the late 12th century in present-day northwestern Iran, and later moved to Anatolia where he worked as a leather merchant. He tried to create the framework for an organisation to assist craftsmen in their trade, and which was named the Ahi Brotherhood after him. According to some sources, Ahi Evran was killed by Mongol invaders in 1261, but his organisation continued to develop.

As the Seljuk state gradually disintegrated under the pressure of the Mongol Empire, small states emerged and occupied parts of the sultanate. Although there were members of the Ahi Brotherhood present in many cities, the Ahi Brotherhood was strongest in the area of present-day Ankara. This significant number, along with the need to preserve peace and the basic functions of the state, led to the declaration of semi-independence of the Ahi Beylik around 1290 under Mongol supreme governance. This beylik was distinct from other states across Anatolia as it was not ruled by a dynasty, but by leaders of the craft guilds. This resembled many European mercantile republics, such as Venice, Genoa, the German free imperial cities, or the Russian city-republics of Novgorod and Pskov, which is why the Ahi Beylik was often called the Ahi Republic. The organisation of the Ahi was partly religious, partly military, and was known for its strong ethics and respect for morality, honesty, and mutual support among its members. As it contributed to the economic development of the entire region, the Republic's power and influence continued to grow steadily.

The development of the Ahi Republic lasted until 1354 when Orhan Ghazi, the second Sultan of the Ottoman Empire, conquered Ankara. After the death of Orhan, the Ahi leaders briefly revived their beylik, but the new Sultan, Orhan's son Murat I, abolished any political influence of the guilds, and the territory of the small free merchant republic was integrated into the flourishing Ottoman Empire.

BEYLIK OF **ALAIYE**

Coastal fortress of independence

LOCATION: Present-day Turkey
PERIOD: 1293–1471
AREA: 100–300 sq km
POPULATION: unknown

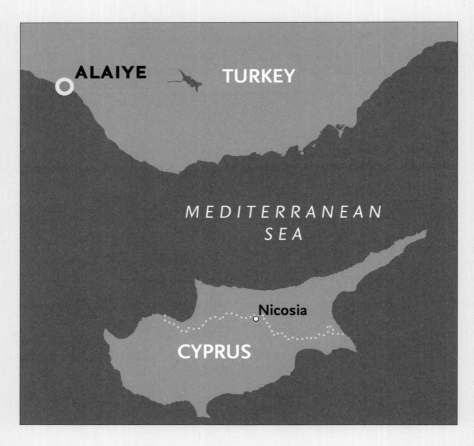

ALAIYE

TURKEY

MEDITERRANEAN SEA

Nicosia

CYPRUS

0   100 km

The Seljuk Sultanate of Rûm was primarily situated in the interior of Anatolia/Asia Minor. Sultan Alā ad-Dīn Kayqubad I took the former Byzantine port of Kalon Oros from the Armenian Kingdom of Cilicia in 1221. Located on the Mediterranean coast, almost facing **Cyprus**, the city was renamed Alaiye in honour of the Sultan. He initiated significant restoration of the city, and the construction of new buildings, including an impressive fortress, the famous Red Tower, and the Yivli Minaret Mosque. The city and its surrounding area were granted the status of a beylik (principality) within the Sultanate of Rûm, and it often served as the capital during winters for the sultans.

The small beylik/principality had a favourable geographical position because its port connected Anatolia with Cyprus, **Syria**, and **Egypt**. However, its relationship with Cyprus was variable, sometimes friendly to mutual benefit and, at other times, hostile.

After the defeat of the Seljuk state by the Mongols in 1243, the Sultanate of Rûm became a vassal of the Mongol Empire. The central government in Anatolia collapsed, and was replaced by a large number of semi-independent beyliks. In 1284, the crusader King of Cyprus tried to take advantage of this situation and attacked Alaiye, conquering the port and Red Tower (Kızıl Kule in Turkish), but failing to seize the fortress. Several years passed before a noble from the neighbouring Beylik of Karaman managed to drive out the crusaders and re-establish the autonomous Beylik of Alaiye in 1293. Despite its relative independence, Alaiye was in a subordinate position to its neighbouring powers, who were militarily stronger: the Beylik of Karaman, the Egyptian Mamluk Sultanate, and the Mongol Ilkhanate. The vassal relationship was mainly not much of a problem, so the city continued to develop, bringing substantial profit to its Bey (leader) and the entire population from timber, silk, and the trade in enslaved people.

The strengthening of the Ottoman Beylik and its conflict with the other powerful local opponent, the Beylik of Karaman, created a significant problem for Alaiye. The Karamanids used this port to receive military aid from the Knights Hospitaller of Rhodes, who gladly helped the enemies of their enemies. In order to prevent this, the Ottomans sent an army to the small coastal beylik. The Bey realised he could not cope win against such a great military force, and in 1471, he surrendered his city without a fight. In return, he received a large estate from the Ottomans near the present-day Greek–Turkish border, and the Beylik of Alaiye ceased to exist, merging into the mighty Ottoman Empire.

According to some sources, centuries later, in the 1930s, Mustafa Kemal Atatürk, founder of the Republic of **Turkey** (also known as Republic of Türkiye) briefly visited Alaiye. After he left, the mayor wanted to thank him for the visit by telegram. However, for some reason, the name of the city was misspelled in the telegram. Unexpectedly, Atatürk liked this new name, so on his suggestion, Alaiye became Alanya, as it is still called today.

Completed in 1226, the Red Tower, or Kızıl Kule,
provided protection both for the coastal city of Alaiye
(now Alanya in present-day Turkey) and for its shipyard.

The towering edifice of the Four Seasons Hotel sits on an island surrounded by the Bahraini capital of Manama and The Gulf.

KINGDOM OF **BAHRAIN**

Desert islands and the Tree of Life

LOCATION: The Gulf
PERIOD: since 1971
AREA: 787 sq km
POPULATION: 1,472,233

SAUDI ARABIA

THE GULF

Um Al Naasan

MANAMA

Mountain of Smoke —▲
134

Gulf of Bahrain

QATAR

Hawar Island

SAUDI ARABIA

0   30 km

The Gulf consists of a large number of islands, mostly belonging to the surrounding mainland countries. The only island country in The Gulf is the Kingdom of **Bahrain**, an archipelago located between **Qatar** and **Saudi Arabia**. Due to land reclamation, the number of islands has doubled, and the small kingdom has increased in size from 665 to over 780 square kilometres. Most of the archipelago is very dry and flat, with the highest peak, the Mountain of Smoke, at only 134 metres above sea level. This peak owes its name to the haze that lingers there during humid periods. Weapons and tools from the Stone Age have been found in numerous caves. The archipelago was occupied by the ancient Dilmun civilisation in 3 BCE. Bahrain was ruled by the Portuguese from the early 16th century until 1602, when it was taken by the Iranian Safavid Empire. In the 17th and 18th centuries, the island was settled by allied tribes from the Arabian Peninsula, led by the ancestors of today's Bahraini royal family.

Bahrain was a protectorate of the **United Kingdom** during most of the 19th and 20th centuries, but gained independence in 1971. Although at this time Iran believed that the small archipelago should belong to it for historical reasons, Shah Reza Pahlavi agreed that the people of Bahrain should hold a referendum. The vast majority favoured independence, thus creating the sovereign State of Bahrain, led by an emir from the Al Khalifa dynasty, which has ruled the archipelago since 1783. The title of emir was replaced by the title of king in 2002, and Bahrain became a semi-constitutional monarchy, granting women the right to vote.

The discovery of large oil reserves in the 1970s significantly boosted the economy of the newly independent state, turning it into a significant business hub in the region. The Lebanese Civil War, which lasted from 1975 to 1990, forced numerous banks to leave Beirut, the former financial centre of the Middle East, and find their new home in Bahrain.

Bahrain, the world's third most densely populated country, currently has nearly 1.5 million inhabitants, of whom only 48% are Bahraini. The ratio of men (61%) to women (39%) is largely due to the numerous male foreign workers who reside alone in Bahrain, without their spouses or families.

The Kingdom of Bahrain is among the fastest-growing economies and financial centres in the world. Agriculture, though, is undeveloped, which is no surprise considering that less than 3% of the country's land is arable. On the other hand, tourism is experiencing a significant boom. Bahrain has the allure of once being the world's largest producer of high quality pearls. Other attractions include its cosmopolitan society; the Bahrain Grand Prix – the only Formula 1 race held in the Middle East; the Bahrain World Trade Centre, a 50-storey building with integrated wind turbines; and numerous festivals. The solitary 'Tree of Life' stands in the midst of the dry desert, 5 kilometres from the Mountain of Smoke. Around 400 years old and 10 metres high, it mysteriously thrives in an area with minimal rainfall or any other significant source of fresh water, providing another tourist attraction and making it symbol of Bahrain's resilience.

FREE **DADRA AND NAGAR HAVELI**

Police shortages and Indian flags

LOCATION: West coast of India
PERIOD: 1954–1961
AREA: 491 sq km
POPULATION: unknown

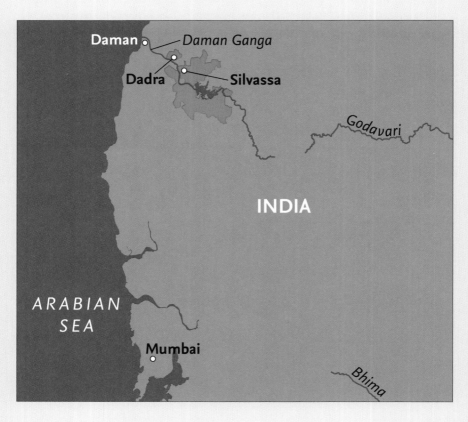

Daman
Daman Ganga
Dadra
Silvassa
Godavari
INDIA
ARABIAN SEA
Mumbai
Bhima

0   50 km

Portuguese **India** (1505–1961) was a state within the Portuguese Empire, consisting of a large number of small and disconnected colonies and fortresses along the entire coast of present-day India. After the Second World War, Portugal lost many of these possessions, retaining only Goa, Daman, and Diu.

Daman consisted of the port of the same name and two nearby mainland enclaves, which had been Portuguese colonies since 1779: the smaller Dadra and the larger Nagar Haveli. When India gained its independence from **Britain** in 1947, the last remnants of Portuguese India found themselves surrounded by the newly created republic. The stance of the Indian authorities was clear – colonial rule needed to be abolished, and the former colonies handed over to the administration of the new state. This was supported by the local population, as well as by most political parties and organisations.

From **Portugal**'s standpoint, the situation did not look bright: the two enclaves were guarded by about 300 policemen, while Indian military forces blocked the arrival of any military aid from Daman port. The Dadra enclave had only three policemen deployed, so was unsurprisingly the first target of Indian activists, who crossed the border on 22 July 1954, and took over the police station. The following day, the Indian flag was hoisted from the police station, and a village council was hastily formed. At the end of the month, the village of Naroli, separated from the rest of the larger Nagar Haveli enclave by the Daman Ganga River, was attacked. The Indian flag flew and a village council was formed immediately. Several tens of thousands of Indian activists proceeded to take over Silvassa, the capital of Nagar Haveli, on 2 August. Free Dadra and Nagar Haveli (FDNH) was declared, a pro-Indian administration elected (Varishta Panchayat of FDNH), and the Indian flag was flown from all public buildings.

From 1954 to 1961, Free Dadra and Nagar Haveli functioned as a de facto independent state. In mid-1961, the administration formally requested accession to India. In order to achieve this, India sent its official who was appointed as the Prime Minister of FDNH on 11 August, with only one task: to sign an agreement with his Indian counterpart, Jawaharlal Nehru, for the official accession of FDNH to the Republic of India. On the same day, an amendment to the Constitution of India was passed, establishing the Union Territory of Dadra and Nagar Haveli.

In late 1961, the army of the Republic of India occupied Goa, Daman, and Diu, the last remnants of Portuguese India. The Union Territory of Goa, Daman and Diu was formed from these territories, which lasted until 1987 when Goa was declared a fully-fledged state of the Indian federation.

In January 2020, the Indian government merged the Union Territories of Dadra and Nagar Haveli and Daman and Diu, creating a new Union Territory with the matter-of-fact name Dadra and Nagar Haveli and Daman and Diu.

DERBENT KHANATE

A much-desired state for Khans and Emperors

LOCATION: Caspian Sea coast
PERIOD: 1747–1806
AREA: c. 700 sq km
POPULATION: C. 10,000

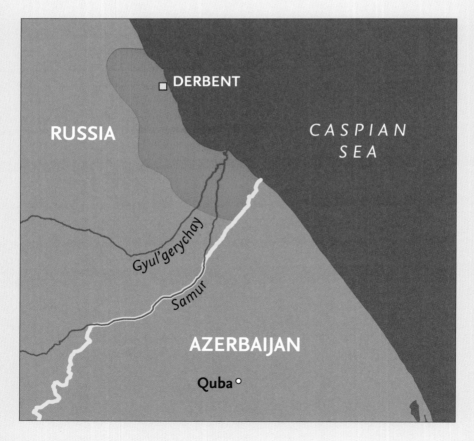

The Caucasus region has always been ethnically and religiously diverse, and due to its significant strategic position, it was of interest to numerous conquerors and surrounding powers. The largest part of Dagestan, presently the southernmost republic within Russia had belonged to Persia from the 16th century. This precursor to modern Iran began losing its power at the beginning of the 18th century, a situation of which Russia took advantage, taking control of the Caucasus region and surrounding areas. The ancient city of Derbent was conquered at that time. The city's name in Persian means 'barrier gate', the barrier being the Caucasus mountain range, and the mighty fortress of Derbent, situated in a narrow coastal plain between the Caucasus and the **Caspian Sea**, serving as the gateway between Europe and Asia.

In order to prevent the destruction of the city, the local leader, Imam Quli Khan, sent its keys to the Russian Emperor Peter I as a sign of submission. The Emperor accepted the peaceful surrender of the city and reappointed Khan as the head of Derbent and its surroundings, laying the foundations for the emergence of a semi-independent khanate several decades later.

In 1735, the balance of power between **Russia** and Persia changed, and Derbent was ceded back under the control of Persia, which was then ruled by the mighty Nader Shah Afshar, the King of Kings, the Sultan of Sultans. After Nader Shah's death in 1747, his state rapidly weakened, and about ten de facto independent khanates emerged in the Caucasus region. One of them was the Derbent Khanate.

The new khan of Derbent, Muhammad Hassan, son of Imam Quli Khan, was not popular among his subjects as he imposed very high taxes. Many residents complained to Fatali Khan, the ruler of the neighbouring Quba Khanate, which he had eagerly anticipated – he had long been looking for a reason to attack and conquer his small northern neighbour. In 1765, he conquered Derbent, united it to his khanate, and blinded the former ruler, keeping him imprisoned in his capital.

Fatali Khan died in 1789, leading to the collapse of his state and gradual re-establishment of Derbent's independence. Hasan Aga, one of Fatali Khan's sons, became head of the khanate in 1799. He died in 1802, and the new ruler of the Quba Khanate once again took control of Derbent, forming a kind of personal union between the two khanates. However, this situation did not last long: by 1806, Russian troops once again occupied Derbent and much of the Caucasus, ending the existence of the Caucasian khanates. Through the Treaty of Gulistan, signed in 1813, Persia ceded the territories of present-day Azerbaijan, Dagestan, and parts of **Georgia** and **Armenia** to Russia.

Derbent is considered one of the oldest continuously inhabited cities in the world, and its mighty walls have withstood the ravages of time, representing a tourist and archaeological attraction.

STATE OF **FREE LEBANON**

Microstate backed by Israel and American Evangelicals

LOCATION: Southern Lebanon
PERIOD: 1979–1984
AREA: c. 240 sq km
POPULATION: c. 100,000

MEDITERRANEAN
SEA

LEBANON

Beirut

SYRIA

Damascus

Bent
Jbaïl

Ramyah

ISRAEL

0   50 km

The bloody civil war in **Lebanon** lasted from 1975 to 1990. The war caused the deaths of thousands of people, destroyed countless buildings, and led to the economic ruin of the country. A similar fate befell the Lebanese armed forces: the army fell apart along ethnic and religious lines. Some officers began gathering soldiers of the same ethnic and/or religious background around them. In 1976, the predominantly Christian Army of Free Lebanon was formed, from which the South Lebanon Army (SLA) was formed the following year (initially named the 'Free Lebanon Army') under the command of former Lebanese Army Major Saad Haddad. He was born into a Greek Catholic family in the southern town of Marjayoûn. Officially, the main goal of this militia was to protect the Maronite Christian population of southern Lebanon, although there were claims that the real aim was to create a buffer zone between **Israel** and its opponents in Lebanon.

Three years later, on 18 April 1979, the independence of the Free State of Lebanon was proclaimed, and Saad Haddad was elected as its president. Immediately afterward, the authorities of Lebanon declared him a traitor and officially dismissed him from the army. Haddad's and the Southern Lebanon Army's authority extended into a narrow strip along the Israeli border, from the Mediterranean Sea almost to the Syrian border, which included his hometown, the 'capital' of Free Lebanon, Marjayoûn. No state recognised the independence of Free Lebanon, although it had military and political support from Israel, as well as material support from some Christian organisations, primarily American Evangelicals. Israel provided significant assistance to this quasi-state by permitting those from southern Lebanon to work legally in Israel and export their goods through the port of Haifa.

Haddad died in his hometown in 1984, and he was succeeded as the commander of the SLA by General Antoine Lahad. The power of Free Lebanon gradually waned, but the militia's influence persisted for another 15 years. The SLA remained firmly allied with Israel until 2000, when Israel decided to withdraw its forces from Lebanon. This decision marked the collapse of the Lebanese militia, which effectively ceased to exist just a few days later.

KINGDOM OF **JAXA**

Polish kingdom in the Far East

LOCATION: Russia–China border, Eastern Asia
PERIOD: 1665–1674
AREA: c. 700 sq km
POPULATION: c. 10,000

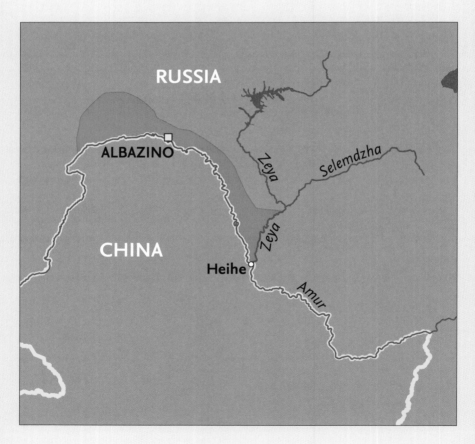

RUSSIA

ALBAZINO

Zeya

Selemdzha

CHINA

Zeya

Heihe

Amur

0   300 km

The eastward expansion of the **Russian Empire** brought many Russians to the distant regions of Siberia. Yerofey Khabarov led a large group of Cossacks in an exploration of the course of the Amur River, and after a conflict with the local Mongolian Daurs in 1651, he established the fort of Albazin (now a village called Albazino, in Russia) on one of the northernmost bends of the Amur. Just a year later, the Chinese conquered and destroyed the fortress, and most of the Russians withdrew from the river area.

Several years passed until a Polish nobleman, Nikifor Romanovich Chernigovsky (or Jaxa-Czernichowski), appeared on the scene. He had been exiled to **Siberia** after the Polish–Russian war ended. While staying with his wife and children in the small Siberian town of Ilimsk, a local *voivode* (military commander) raped his daughter. Nikifor murdered the voivode and fled to the remote regions around the Amur River, where the Russian authorities could not reach and punish him. Together with a group of 84 Cossacks and a priest, he reached the ruins of the former fortress of Albazin. They decided to settle there in 1665 and rebuild the fortress, which Nikifor named Jaxa (pronounced: Yaxa), after the griffin (Polish: *gryf* or *jaxa*) on his family coat of arms.

Nikifor quickly established good relations with the surrounding indigenous Daur and Evenk people with whom he traded successfully. As word on the new fortress spread across Siberia, more and more Cossacks joined the Polish nobleman, who considered himself the King of his small town. The Cossacks supported this, and the Daurs and Evenks began to bring gifts to the new ruler in return for protection from occasional Chinese incursions. The new microstate was relatively prosperous, despite several attempts by Russian Siberian governors to stand in the way of the small Polish kingdom in the Far East. Much of this was due to the wise policy of Chernigovsky: he fought against the Russians using the Chinese, and against the Chinese using the Russians. However, he knew very well that he would have to align with one side to survive in this distant inhospitable region. So, from 1669, he began to send tribute to the Russian imperial court, thus acknowledging the supreme Russian authority. The Tsar accepted this, and in 1674 proclaimed Nikifor as the Lord of Jaxa. Although the Chinese imperial government respected the small neighbour and communicated with Jaxa in Polish, Chernigovsky attacked neighbouring Chinese territories with his Cossacks in 1675, allegedly to aid his Daur subjects. This was the last recorded reference to him, so it is presumed that he died during that mission.

His city endured for some time, but the Chinese finally conquered and destroyed it in 1685. After surrendering, a group of Russian defenders decided to relocate, which is why there is a population of several hundred Albazinians, a small ethnically Russian group of Orthodox faith, now living in **China**. Over time, they stopped using the Russian language, and through mixing with the local population, they lost the physical characteristics of Russians, but retained their faith even during the Chinese 'cultural revolution'.

KINGDOM OF **KUBANG PASU DARUL QIYAM**

From hero king to zero king

LOCATION: Southeast Asia
PERIOD: 1839–1859
AREA: 900 sq km
POPULATION: unknown

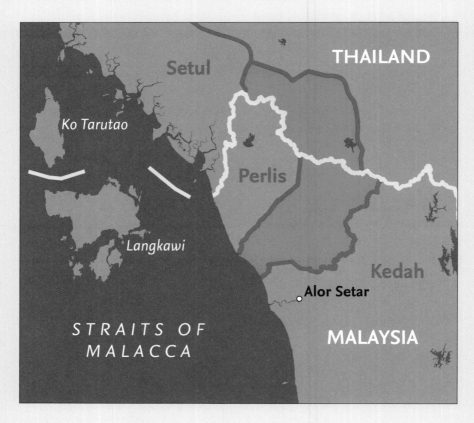

After conflicts between the Kingdom of Siam (modern-day **Thailand**) and its vassal state, the Kedah Sultanate (now a federal state within **Malaysia**), Siam successfully attacked Kedah in 1821, establishing direct control over the rebellious sultanate. The Sultan was forced into exile, from which he made several unsuccessful attempts to launch a struggle for the liberation of Kedah. However, Tunku Anum, the son of the governor of one of Kedah's provinces, had a cunning plan up his sleeve. He managed to become friends with the new Siamese governor of Kedah while simultaneously preparing a rebel army to fight against the occupiers. The struggle began and, as a result of health problems among the Siamese soldiers and the high costs of war, Siam was forced to withdraw from Kedah, which regained self-government in 1842, although formally remaining a vassal of Siam.

To demonstrate its submission, every three years Kedah had to send tribute to Siam, known as *bunga mas* ('golden flower'), in the form of two small trees made of silver and gold along with additional valuable gifts (jewellery, tobacco, weapons). On the other hand, the Sultan was allowed to return from years of exile. In gratitude, the Sultan bestowed upon Tunku Anum a small territory, which officially became the Kingdom of Kubang Pasu Darul Qiyam, known as Kubang Pasu (*Darul Qiyam* can be translated as 'independent state').

Tunku Anum's accession to the throne of the small kingdom marked the beginning of a golden era that lasted throughout his 17-year reign. Kubang Pasu became the centre for rice cultivation, a strategically important commodity. The river control system was improved; textile factories, a fort, courts, and schools were built; and Kampung Pulau Pisang, the capital of the new kingdom, became a centre of significant trade.

After the death of Tunku Anum in 1853, his grandson Tunku Ishak became King of Kubang Pasu (Anum's son, and Ishak's father, had died in 1848). Unfortunately, Ishak was the complete opposite of his grandfather – his cruel rule and poor state policies made him unpopular among the population. Under pressure from dissatisfied subjects, Tunku Ishak abdicated the throne in 1859, and his Kingdom once again became part of the Sultanate of Kedah.

Today Kubang Pasu is a district of the Malaysian federal state of Kedah, with almost the same borders as in the mid-19th century, when it was a semi-independent kingdom. Unfortunately, over time, almost all traces of this once successful microstate have disappeared. Perhaps the most visible reminder of that former time is the tomb of the King-hero Tunku Anum in Pulau Pisang, now part of Jitra, the modern capital of Kubang Pasu District in Malaysia.

KINGDOM OF **LO**

The rooftop of the world

LOCATION: present-day Nepal
PERIOD: 1380–2008
AREA: c. 2,000 sq km
POPULATION: c. 2,000

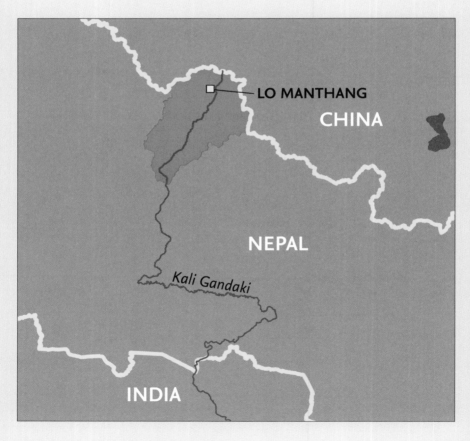

High up on the roof of the world, amidst the towering peaks of the Himalaya, lies the region of Upper Mustang, a part of the Tibetan Plateau. Surrounded by the mighty mountains of Dhaulagiri (8,167 metres) and Annapurna (8,091 metres), Upper Mustang represents an extremely dry, cold, and inhospitable place to live. However, its strategic location on the trade route between Tibet (now an autonomous region in **China**) and **India**, used for transporting valuable loads of salt, led to the creation of a small kingdom in 1380, under the leadership of the legendary hero and king, Ame Pal. He named his land Lo, meaning 'South' (of the rest of Tibet). Linguistic and cultural ties with Tibet were, and still are, very strong and unbreakable. Ame Pal ordered the construction of Lo Manthang, with the capital surrounded by sturdy walls, which has not much changed to this day. Numerous Buddhist temples were built in the centuries that followed, and Buddhism became the foundation of life for the people of the Kingdom of Lo (alternatively known as Mustang, from the Tibetan word *möntang*, meaning 'fertile plain', although only barley and buckwheat thrive here).

At the end of the 18th century, the ruler of the Kingdom of Gorkha, Prithvi Narayan Shah, united numerous small states under his rule, including Lo, laying the foundation for the creation of modern Nepal. Since 1795, Lo had been a vassal of predominantly Hindu Nepal, but still with broad internal self-government. This remained mostly unchanged for a century and a half, but in the years following the annexation of Tibet by the People's Republic of China in 1951, Upper Mustang became the centre of Tibetan guerrilla activity. After the situation stabilised, the small Himalayan Kingdom became a restricted area, with the hope of protecting its way of life, Tibetan language, and Buddhist religion.

A significant political change occurred in Nepal in 2008: the Kingdom was abolished and replaced with a democratic federal republic. This marked the end of all tributary states and territories, including the Kingdom of Lo. The monarchy ended, and Lo (Upper Mustang) became part of the Mustang district. The last ruler, Jigme Dorje Palbar Bista, was King from 1964 to 2008, but the local population regarded him as their ruler until his death in 2016. He was a direct descendant of Ame Pal and Songtsen Gampo, the greatest King of Tibet from the 7th century.

The entire Mustang region is rich in Buddhist cultural symbols and represents Tibet in miniature. One event which draws tourists is the three-day annual Tiji festival (derived from *Tempa Chirim*, which means 'Prayer for World Peace' in Tibetan), which celebrates the victory of the incarnation of Buddha over the demon who terrorised the land and people.

The Mustang Caves (Sky Caves of Nepal) are located in Mustang, consisting of 10,000 man-made caves where mummified human bodies, over 3,000 years old, have been found, as well as a large number of valuable Buddhist paintings and manuscripts. It is currently unknown who built this vast number of caves, when they built them, and why. One theory suggests that the caves were used as tombs in ancient times, later as shelters from frequent military conflicts, and ultimately as meditation chambers.

This house front is in the former Kingdom of Lo in present-day Nepal. Due to being a restricted area until the 1990s, it is one of the most preserved traditional regions in the world.

The Grand Friday Mosque in Male' is the largest mosque in the Maldives. Built of white marble and opened in 1984, it can accommodate more than 5,000 worshippers.

REPUBLIC OF **MALDIVES**

Land of sea and 12,000 islands

LOCATION: Indian Ocean
PERIOD: since 1965
AREA: 298 sq km
POPULATION: 523,787

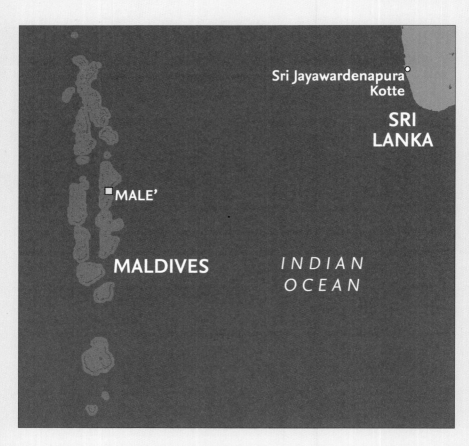

Sri Jayawardenapura Kotte

SRI LANKA

MALE'

MALDIVES

INDIAN OCEAN

0   300 km

The Maldives is an archipelago of around 1,200 small coral islands (the largest being about 8 square kilometres) stretching approximately 850 kilometres from north to south in the middle of the Indian Ocean. **Germany** is approximately the same extent from its northernmost to southernmost points. However, the difference between these two countries lies in the surface area: the Maldives covers about 300 square kilometres, while Germany, at 360,000 square kilometres, is around 1,200 times larger. It is no surprise that the Maldives is the country with the smallest surface area in the largest continent – Asia. This island country is also the lowest in the world, with the highest natural point in the archipelago only 2 metres above sea level. Climate change and rising sea levels pose a significant threat to the future of the Maldives.

It is assumed that more than 40 centuries ago, the archipelago was first settled by people originating from the vicinity of the northwestern Indian city of Kalibangan, not far from the border with Pakistan. The first small island states were recorded around the 5th century BCE, and numerous artifacts show the presence of Hinduism. In the 3rd century BCE, there was a marked religious change when the majority of Maldivians embraced Buddhism. The situation would change again 1,500 years later when the Buddhist King, Dhovemi, converted to Islam, becoming Sultan Muhammad al-Adil in the second half of the 12th century. His successors officially used the extensive title Sultan of Land and Sea, Lord of the 12,000 Islands (although there are only about 1,200 islands), and Sultan of the **Maldives**. Since then, the Maldives has almost exclusively been a Muslim country, with followers of this religion making up about 99% of the population. In 2008, Islam was declared the state religion, alongside a ban on the public practice of other religions. The constitution clearly states that when something is not defined by law, judges should apply the rules of Islamic Shari'ah. However, foreign tourists are not prohibited from adhering to their religious rules and beliefs, where these are different.

Today, there is a great number of foreign tourists, and almost one third of the gross domestic product comes from this sector of the economy. The development of tourism in the Maldives began only in the early 1970s. Until then, the Maldives was among the poorest countries in the world, with income mostly derived from fishing and the sale of coconut rope, ambergris (a product from the digestive tract of sperm whales, used in cosmetics), and giant coco de mer palm fruits, to countries in South and East Asia.

The majority of the Maldivian population and the neighbouring Indian island of Minicoy belong to the ethnic group Dhivehin (the Maldivians). They write their language using a script known as Thaana, developed in the 17th century, which is unique in that the order of the letters follows no logical pattern.

NORTH SENTINEL
ISLAND

*An isolated and
forbidden land*

LOCATION: Andaman Islands, Indian Ocean
PERIOD: since 48000 BCE
AREA: 60 sq km
POPULATION: 15–500

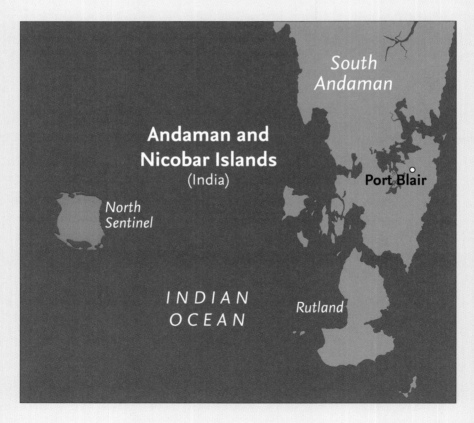

South
Andaman

**Andaman and
Nicobar Islands**
(India)

Port Blair

North
Sentinel

*INDIAN
OCEAN*

Rutland

0   20 km

India is a federal republic comprising 28 states and 8 union territories. States have their own governments, while union territories are governed centrally. Although each of the states and union territories has its own characteristics, the union territory of Andaman and Nicobar Islands stands out from all the rest. Within this archipelago lies an island that can be viewed as a kind of independent state, whose inhabitants have been purposefully avoiding any contact with the outside world for millennia.

The island in question is known to India and the rest of the world as North Sentinel, and its people are known as the Sentinelese. It is unknown to us what the inhabitants of that island call their island or themselves. It is believed that the Sentinelese have been living there for more than 50,000 years, meaning they were direct descendants of the first human population that left Africa about 80–100,000 years ago and headed round the southern coast of Asia towards **Australia**. The population figure is based solely on observation from a distance, and estimates can range from anywhere between 15 and 500 people. Their language is also completely unknown to us; we only know that people from neighbouring islands, who have had the opportunity to hear the Sentinelese speak, found their language to be incomprehensible.

North Sentinel is roughly square shaped, 8 kilometres in length and 7 kilometres in width. The entire island, other than the narrow shore, is forested. It is inhabited by large numbers of wild boars, coconut crabs, and sea turtles, which are a major food source for the Sentinelese. The highest elevation is estimated to be around 120 metres. The island is surrounded by coral reefs, which makes it difficult for ships to approach. There used to be a forested islet located about 600 metres from North Sentinel, but the earthquake that caused the devastating tsunami in 2004 raised both islands by 1–2 metres and merged them.

In recent history, there have been several attempts to contact the Sentinelese, but most have ended badly, often with the killing of unwanted intruders. To prevent future potentially bloody conflicts, and to protect the Sentinelese from modern diseases to which they have no immunity, the Indian government decided that North Sentinel and its surrounding waters would become a prohibited area for visits. Since Indian government authorities have no control over the island or its population, North Sentinel can be viewed as an independent state under India's protection, or as a protectorate. Even in extreme cases when uninvited guests have been killed, neither India nor any other state has ever retaliated against the Sentinelese.

Parallels have been drawn between the Sentinelese and people of the Stone Age era, which is not an accurate comparison. For example, it is known that they use metal parts from shipwrecks to make weapons and arrowheads. Despite living on an isolated island, it can be concluded from the few encounters that have occurred so far that the Sentinelese are fairly healthy and want only one thing: to be left alone on their small, green island, far from the everyday problems of the rest of the world.

REPUBLIC OF **PALAU**

Jellyfish Lake and ghost capital

LOCATION: Western Pacific Ocean
PERIOD: since 1981
AREA: 497 sq km
POPULATION: 18,055

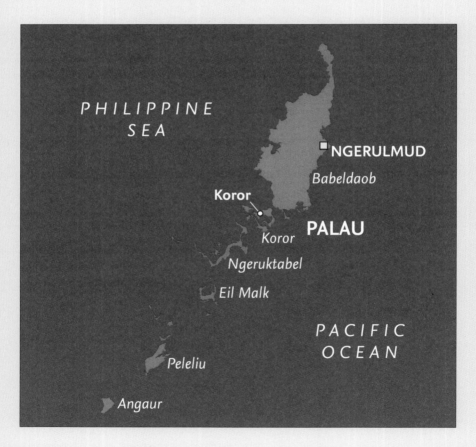

PHILIPPINE SEA

NGERULMUD

Babeldaob

Koror

Koror

PALAU

Ngeruktabel

Eil Malk

PACIFIC OCEAN

Peleliu

Angaur

0   30 km

The capital city is often the largest settlement of a country or, if not the largest, it is usually the centre of state power. However, Ngerulmud, the capital of the Republic of Palau, an island nation in the western Pacific, differs from this model. The most prominent building in Ngerulmud is the Capitol of Palau, a magnificent palace housing the Palau National Congress (in Palauan: *Olbiil era Kelulau*), the government, the president of the state, and the Supreme Court. Around this complex there is a beautiful, dense forest, a modern road... and nothing more. There are no residential buildings or houses because, according to official data, Ngerulmud has zero permanent residents. How did this unusual situation come about?

It is presumed that Palau's first inhabitants, originating from present-day Indonesia, settled there around 2000 BCE. In the 19th century, the archipelago was annexed to the Spanish colony of the Philippines, but was sold to Germany at the end of that century. Japan took control of the islands from the beginning of the First World War until the end of the Second World War, when they were conquered by the **United States** in a very bloody conflict. By adopting a new constitution, Palau became an independent republic in 1981. The following year, it signed the Compact of Free Association with the United States, through which the United States effectively gained defence and military control over Palau, while Palau, in return, received financial and other assistance necessary for the development of its state independence.

Upon gaining independence, Koror, the largest city in Palau, was designated as the temporary capital, with the constitution stating that the permanent capital would be established on Babeldaob (the largest island), within ten years of ratification. When it was time to relocate the capital, the authorities of Palau did not choose any of the existing populated places but instead designated a hilltop on Babeldaob as the location for the new Capitol of Palau, whose appearance bears a significant resemblance to the American Capitol. Thus, Ngerulmud, the capital city without a single resident, was created.

Palau consists of 16 states (with functions similar to municipalities), most of which have fewer than 500 inhabitants, with the smallest, Hatohobei, having a population of just 25. In the north of Babeldaob Island lies the state of Ngarchelong, covering an area of 10 square kilometres and with fewer than 400 inhabitants. This state is home to the Badrulchau Stone Monoliths, a collection of about twenty (or, according to some sources, fifty) stone monoliths over 2 metres high and spread over an area of about 2 hectares. There is currently not enough knowledge about the purpose of these monoliths, but it is believed they were carved around the year 150 CE.

On Eil Malk Island (also known as Mecherchar), there is an unusual saline lake, known as Jellyfish Lake, which is home to millions of jellyfish and is an interesting tourist destination. The lake is notable for having almost no oxygen at depths greater than 15 metres and being full of potentially dangerous hydrogen sulphide.

BYZANTINE
PHILADELPHIA

The city of brotherly love

LOCATION: Aegean region of Turkey
PERIOD: 1310–1390
AREA: a few dozen sq km
POPULATION: 18,000

The collapse of the Sultanate of Rûm at the start of the 14th century opened the possibility for the creation of many small Turkish beyliks, which, as well as fighting amongst themselves, also gradually carved away parts of the declining **Byzantine Empire**.

During the two decades that followed the Sultanate's collapse, these beyliks seized large parts of Asia Minor, leaving only a narrow strip along the coast of the Sea of Marmara, with the former capitals of Nicaea and Nicomedia, under the control of the emperors of Constantinople. However, far in the south, the city of Philadelphia persisted as a kind of Hellenistic-Christian settlement amidst the vast (and encroaching) Turkish-Muslim sea. After 1310, this enclave became a vassal of the then-powerful Germiyan Beylik.

Philadelphia was known as one of the Seven Churches of Revelation mentioned in the New Testament's Book of Revelation, and as a city where Christianity had taken root as early as the middle of the 1st century. It owed its freedom to its mighty walls, its remote location among the mountains of the Lydia region, and its willingness to pay *jizyah* (a tax non-Muslim inhabitants paid to Muslim rulers) to the surrounding Turkish beyliks. Philadelphia could not rely on aid from Byzantium, as the Empire's border was receding further whilst the surrounding beyliks expanded. The Ottoman Beylik represented a particular threat to Byzantium, as it was already threatening the shores of the Sea of Marmara and Nicaea. In order to counter the Ottomans, the Byzantine Emperor Andronikos III launched a military offensive against them, but the Turkish Sultan Orhan Gazi achieved a significant victory near the besieged Nicomedia, further weakening the Byzantine position in Asia Minor.

The Turks conquered Nicaea in 1331 and Nicomedia in 1337. From that moment, Philadelphia remained the only territory in Asia Minor under Byzantine rule. However, due to its distance from the home state and the coast, Philadelphia functioned mostly as an independent state, for a time under the influence of the Knights of Rhodes. Left on its own, the 'City of Brotherly Love' (which is the original meaning of the word 'Philadelphia') began independently to negotiate agreements and alliances with the surrounding beyliks.

At one point, rival pretenders to the imperial throne in Constantinople sought help from the Ottomans, promising in return that Philadelphia would surrender. However, the inhabitants of Philadelphia rejected this, so the Ottoman Sultan Bayezid the Thunderbolt began a siege of the city in 1390, allegedly aided by subordinate co-emperors of the Byzantine Empire. The story goes that the Philadelphians decided to surrender without a fight when they saw the Byzantine imperial flag among the attackers. The fall of the distant Philadelphia had little impact on Byzantium, as it had long lost sovereignty over Asia Minor.

Today, Philadelphia is the Turkish city of **Alaşehir**, known for grape cultivation and its rich cultural and historical heritage.

REPUBLIC OF
SINGAPORE

City of lions

LOCATION: Southeast Asia
PERIOD: since 1965
AREA: 736 sq km
POPULATION: 5,975,689

MALAYSIA

SINGAPORE

STRAIT OF
SINGAPORE

INDONESIA

0   20 km

Singapore is a city-state located just 137 kilometres north of the Equator, off the southern tip of the Malay Peninsula. It is one of the most developed countries in the world, with very low levels of corruption and high levels of education and healthcare. Numerous strict laws and regulations contribute to the quality of life and the maintenance of such a small territory. One famous rule prohibits the import and sale of chewing gum (except for medical purposes), which is justified by the high costs of cleaning improperly disposed-of gum.

Singapore consists of about 60 islands, but through the process of land reclamation, the total area of the state increased from 580 square kilometres in the 1960s to 736 in 2023. The formation of additional islands is planned. Despite high levels of urbanisation, the Singapore authorities strive to create as many green areas and parks as possible for their residents. One such park is the Night Safari, the world's first nocturnal zoo, where visitors can observe the nighttime behaviour of animals, separated from humans by natural barriers, rather than by conventional fences and cages. Gardens by the Bay is another nature park, covering an area of over 100 hectares, featuring the Flower Dome, the world's largest greenhouse, and the Supertree Grove, an unusual collection of artificial trees with a bridge connecting the two largest.

It is believed that the Kingdom of Singapore was founded in 1299. The name in Sanskrit means 'City of Lions', as the first ruler allegedly saw a lion in the bushes (though it was more likely to have been a tiger, as lions did not live anywhere nearby at that time). Approximately a hundred years later, the Kingdom was attacked by the **Majapahit Empire**, a Hindu-Buddhist state from Java. The King fled to the Malay Peninsula, where he founded the powerful Malacca Sultanate in the following years. In the first half of the 19th century, Singapore became a British colony, and the development of its port began – today one of the busiest in the world. Between 1826 and 1946, Singapore, together with Penang, Malacca, and Dindings, was part, and capital, of the British Straits Settlements colony. Singapore gained full internal self-governance in 1959, and in 1963 united with the Federation of Malaya, North Borneo (Sabah), and Sarawak to form Malaysia. Constant disagreements with the federal government led to Singapore's expulsion from the federation in 1965, creating the independent Republic of Singapore.

Today, Singapore has a population of about 6 million people, of whom 62% are citizens of the city-state. Three-quarters of the population are of Chinese descent, around 13% are Malay, and 9% are Indian. At 31%, Buddhism is the most prevalent religion, followed by Christianity (around 19%) and Islam (15%). Besides being multinational and multiconfessional, Singapore is also a multilingual country, with four official languages: English, Chinese (Mandarin), Malay, and Tamil. English is effectively the main language, while the constitution defines Malay as the national language. However, an increasing number of Singaporeans often use Singlish, especially with family and friends, which is a mixture of all four official languages.

UNITED SUVADIVE
REPUBLIC

Three stars for three atolls

LOCATION: Indian Ocean
PERIOD: 1959–1963
AREA: 58 sq km
POPULATION: 20,000

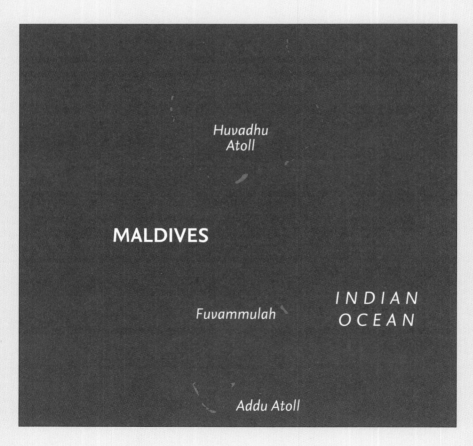

Huvadhu
Atoll

MALDIVES

Fuvammulah

*INDIAN
OCEAN*

Addu Atoll

0   50 km

When a distant region feels neglected by the home state, it can lead to violent protests, conflicts, and even secession. This is precisely what happened in the final years of British influence over the **Maldives**, when the three southernmost atolls of the archipelago declared independence in the form of a new state, the United Suvadive Islands (or United Suvadive Republic, as it is commonly known today).

In the last days of 1958, the government of the Sultanate of the Maldives decided to impose a new boat tax on the residents of its almost 1,200 islands. This, along with almost non-existent healthcare, a lack of schools, and high food prices, sparked massive protests in Hithadhoo, the administrative centre of the southernmost atoll, Addu. Government institutions on the island were attacked, and their officials sought refuge within the British military base. The situation quickly escalated when, in early January 1959, representatives of the demonstrators reached the British airport, where they informed the authorities that the 15-square-kilometre atoll was declaring independence. Soon afterwards, a local government based on democratic principles was elected, focusing on economic development and combating corruption. Two nearby atolls, Fuvammulah (5 square kilometres) and Huvadhu (38 square kilometres, and the largest atoll in the world, consisting of over 250 islands), realised that they would be better off in an alliance with Addu, so in mid-March, they declared secession from the Sultanate and together formed the United Suvadive Islands. A new flag with three stars symbolising the three atolls was chosen. The newly created state was separated from the rest of the Maldives by the Suvadiva Channel (or One and a Half Degree Channel), locally known as Huvadhu Kandu.

Within a few months, the Maldives responded harshly. An armed gunboat under the command of the Sultanate's prime minister quelled the rebellion on Huvadhu Atoll, but Addu avoided such a fate, likely due to the presence of British military forces at Gan airport. After a period of calm, new protests erupted on Huvadhu in 1961. A repeated military coup by the Maldives government, again under the command of Prime Minister Ibrahim Nasir, was much more brutal. Thinadhoo, the wealthy capital of Huvadhu Atoll, located on the island of the same name, was attacked. Almost all buildings on the island were destroyed and burned; all 6,000 residents were displaced to other islands of the archipelago and were not allowed to return until four years later. Many ended up in prisons, where they were tortured, and several Suvadive leaders died behind bars.

Following these events, the British supported the official authorities of the Maldives. The president of the short-lived United Suvadive Republic was evacuated to the Seychelles in 1963, and his state ceased to exist. The Sultan of the Maldives issued an order that none of the participants in the rebellion were to be punished after these events.

Although short-lived, the United Suvadive Republic left its mark on the archipelago by issuing the first passport issued by any part of the present-day Maldives, and establishing the first local bank, in Addu in 1961.

STATE OF **UPPER YAFA**

A sheikhdom with a puppet sultan

LOCATION: Yemen
PERIOD: 1800–1967
AREA: c. 1,000 sq km
POPULATION: c. 35,000

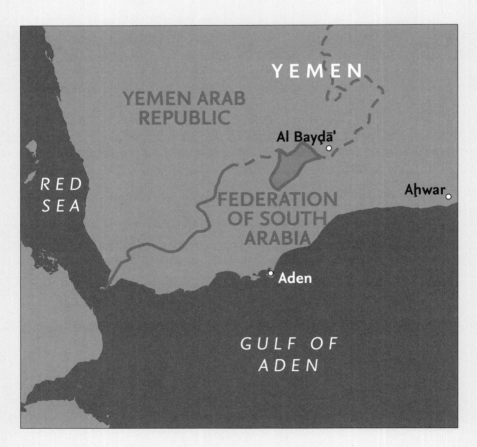

0   100 km

Securing the sea route from Europe, through the Suez Canal, to India was of strategic importance for the British Empire. In order to ensure the safety of the Colony of Aden and its port at the entrance to the Red Sea, **Britain** began making protection agreements with tribal leaders, small sheikhdoms, and sultanates in the southern Arabian Peninsula, now **Yemen**, in the late 19th century. Tribal leaders, sheikhs, and sultans would gain a powerful protector, while retaining a high level of internal autonomy within the British Aden Protectorate; while the British gained control over the entire area of the port of Aden.

Upper Yafa was one of the sultanates that signed the protectorate agreement. This feudal state was located in the mountainous region northeast of Aden and consisted of several autonomous sheikhdoms. Its foundations were laid in the 18th century when the Upper Yafa Sheikhdom was established, whose ruler took the title of sultan in the early 19th century. Despite the distinguished title, the formally subordinate sheikhs paid little attention to their sultan, except in times of military crisis, so Upper Yafa functioned largely as a loose confederation, or military alliance, with each sheikh separately signing a protection agreement with Britain.

These agreements changed very little in the daily life of the small sultanate. The British documented visits to this remote hinterland only a few times, and Upper Yafa continued to function as an independent state (or at least, as a federation of independent states). When Britain decided to bring its protectorates in southern Arabia a little closer to the Federation of the Emirates of the South (1959–1962 – later becoming the **Federation of South Arabia**, 1962–1967), Upper Yafa refused to join that union. After some hesitation, the microstate decided to join the Protectorate of South Arabia as a separate enclave. This was a community of more conservative protectorate states located in the eastern Yemeni historical region of Hadhramaut. The rapid awakening of Arab national consciousness led to the collapse of British colonial policy on the Arabian Peninsula. In 1967, Britain withdrew all its military troops from the region, leading to the merging of the Federation of South Arabia and the Protectorate of South Arabia, which became a new independent socialist state, South Yemen. All sultanates and sheikhdoms were abolished, and many of their rulers left the newly created country.

The Yafa'a tribe remains one of the larger tribes of the Republic of Yemen, formed by the unification of North and South Yemen in 1990. It is believed that this tribe traces its origins to the Himyarites, who ruled the ancient Himyarite Kingdom, a powerful state whose army had conquered the famous Sabean Kingdom in 280 CE. The Himyarites spoke the Himyaritic language, one of the Old South Arabian languages (related to Arabic), with their own script. Initially, they practised South Arabian polytheism, converting to Judaism around 390 CE, and later to Christianity after 500 CE. Islam arrived in Yemen in 630 CE, establishing a firm stronghold that remains to this day.

REPUBLIC OF
ZAMBOANGA

One man's stance against colonial rule

LOCATION: Philippines
PERIOD: 1899–1903
AREA: c. 1,400 sq km
POPULATION: c. 20,000

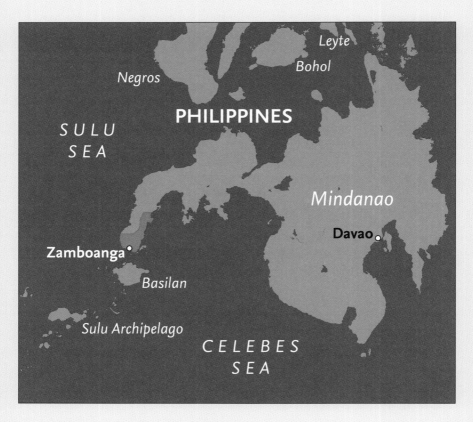

The end of the 19th century saw the rapid demise of the once-powerful **Spanish Empire**, as its colonies liberated themselves one by one from Spanish military authority. One of the last colonies was the **Philippines**, a large group of islands between Indonesia and **China**. A revolutionary uprising erupted across the Philippines in 1896, and in 1898 the archipelago freed itself from Spanish rule after 333 years. The Philippines declared independence the same year, however not only did Spain not recognise this, it sold the rebellious colony to a new master: the United States.

These events did not stop the revolutionary struggle in all parts of the Philippines. In the westernmost part of the island of Mindanao, the second largest in the archipelago of over 7,000 islands, stood the fortress of Fort Pilar (full name: Real Fuerte de Nuestra Señora del Pilar de Zaragoza). There, behind the strong walls of the fortress located in the city of Zamboanga, was where the Spanish governor of the Philippines found refuge, having fled the now United States-controlled capital, Manila. But he could not rest for long, as a group of prominent Zamboangueños (residents of Zamboanga) decided to extend the revolution to the city, and drive out the governor and the Spanish army. The revolutionary army demonstrated the solidarity of all the region's inhabitants, regardless of faith or wealth, and the local population fought in union.

The Zamboanga Peninsula quickly fell into the hands of the revolutionaries, but the sturdy walls of Fort Pilar posed a greater challenge. General Vicente Álvarez, commander of the Revolutionary Government of Zamboanga, ordered the siege of the city. After a month, on 18 May 1899, the Spaniards surrendered and left the city. At the same time, General Álvarez and his associates declared the independence of the Republic of Zamboanga, and Álvarez become the first and only elected president. In theory, the newly formed state included the islands of Mindanao, Sulu, and Basilan, but in reality, it comprised only the city of Zamboanga and its immediate vicinity.

Meanwhile, the Americans had grouped around Zamboanga and, through the 'carrot and stick' approach, persuaded Isidoro Midel, one of President Álvarez's closest collaborators, to betray him. Six months after the declaration of independence, the United States occupied the small republic, forcing Álvarez to flee the city, though he continued a guerrilla struggle until his arrest in 1902. The United States declared Zamboanga its protectorate, appointing Midel as the new president. By 1903, the protectorate was abolished, and Zamboanga was annexed to the colony of the Philippines and designated as the capital of the new Moro province. Álvarez was later released from prison and appointed Vice-Governor of the Zamboanga District.

In the modern era, the city of Zamboanga, in gratitude to General and President Álvarez, bestowed on him the title of 'revolutionary hero', and named a square and street after him. One unique feature of this Philippine city is that it is the only city in Asia where the majority of the population speaks a Spanish-Creole language, Chavanco. Probably the oldest language of its kind, Chavanco is quite similar to Spanish and evolved by mixing Spanish words with local Filipino grammar, making it reminiscent of the the the mixing of revolutionary army of President Álvarez.

OCEANIA

The arrival of 19th-century missionaries to the volcanic island of Bora Bora influenced the island's history by blending new religious practices with Polynesian traditions.

KINGDOM OF **BORA BORA**

Haven of nature and missionaries

LOCATION: Polynesia, South Pacific Ocean
PERIOD: early 19th century–1895
AREA: c. 60 sq km
POPULATION: c. 2,000

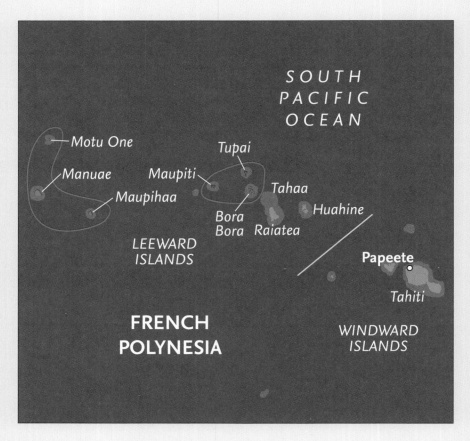

SOUTH PACIFIC OCEAN

Motu One

Tupai

Manuae

Maupiti

Maupihaa

Tahaa

Bora Bora

Huahine

Raiatea

LEEWARD ISLANDS

Papeete

FRENCH POLYNESIA

Tahiti

WINDWARD ISLANDS

0   200 km

When the first Polynesian settlers arrived at the Island of Bora Bora in the 3rd century, they may have thought they had arrived in heaven on Earth. The island was blessed with dense green vegetation, beautiful sandy beaches, a lagoon, and the surrounding sea was rich in marine life – what more could an explorer wish for? Needless to say, the Europeans also recognised its value, when they 'discovered' the islands of **Polynesia**, including Bora Bora, at the end of the 18th century.

During the 18th century, there was a smouldering conflict between **France** and **Britain** over who was to rule these tiny isles scattered across the Pacific Ocean. Apart from the political and military balancing of power, religion also got in the way, so both (French) Catholic and (British) Protestant missionaries stood toe to toe with each other. At the beginning of the 19th century, the island of Bora Bora united with several neighbouring smaller islands, thus (unofficially) establishing the Kingdom of Bora Bora. When the British Protestant missionary in **Tahiti** finally managed to persuade the local Queen to expel his Catholic counterpart, the French expelled the British missionary, and in 1842 Tahiti was declared a French protectorate. Fortunately for the tiny Kingdom of Bora Bora, that island managed to maintain its de facto independence, presumably an attempt by the French to keep the peace with the British. In order to prevent further conflict between the two European superpowers, Britain and France signed the Jarnac Convention in 1847, which recognised the independence of Bora Bora and several neighbouring kingdoms. This convention emphasised that the signatories would neither annex, nor make a protectorate of the island kingdom known collectively as the Leeward Islands (in French: Îles Sous le Vent), and that this agreement would be valid for at least 40 years.

This would have been an opportunity for a period of peace and prosperity, had it not been for the appearance of a third European power, one that was not bound by the Jarnac Convention. This was **Germany**, which belatedly entered the 'market' of colonies, and hastily sought to occupy whatever it could. When the island states of Raiatea and Tahaa voluntarily sought French protection in 1880 against an increasingly aggressive Germany, the French agreed, as they certainly did not want a German colony in their backyard. Thus, the Jarnac convention ceased to exist. France took advantage of this and, in 1887, officially annexed all of the Leeward Islands. At that time, Bora Bora was ruled by Teriimaevarua III, who had ascended the throne in 1873. After the French seizure of her kingdom, she remained Queen but now ruled on behalf of the European colonial power. She voluntarily abdicated in the last years of the 19th century, retaining her title as head of the royal house of Bora Bora until her death in the royal palace in 1932.

COOK ISLANDS

Marine conservation and trading in triangles

LOCATION: Polynesia, South Pacific Ocean
PERIOD: since 1965
AREA: 293 sq km
POPULATION: 17,011

Palmerston

SOUTHERN
GROUP

Aitutaki

Manuae

Mitiaro

**COOK
ISLANDS**

Atiu

Mauke

AVARUA
Rarotonga

SOUTH
PACIFIC
OCEAN

Mangaia

0   200 km

The Cook Islands are located between **American Samoa** and **French Polynesia**. The fifteen islands are divided into two groups, the Northern Group and the Southern Group. The Southern Group contains the territory's largest island, Rarotonga, which is where the capital, Avarua, is located.

It is believed that the ancient Tahitians sailed nearly 1,200 kilometres to settle on the Cook Islands around the year 1000. The first Europeans to sight the islands were the Spanish in 1595, and the British captain James Cook, after whom the archipelago was later named, visited and mapped the islands in the late 18th century, all except Rarotonga.

When the French conquered Tahiti in the mid-19th century, the chiefs of the tribes on Rarotonga and the surrounding islands sought protection from the British, but did not receive a response. At that time, Rarotonga was a fairly wealthy and prosperous kingdom ruled by Queen Makea Takau, the leader of the most influential tribe on the island since 1871. She repeated the request to the British in 1888, who this time responded positively, and most of today's Cook Islands become a British protectorate. After Aitutaki island was annexed in 1891, the protectorate was renamed the Cook Islands Federation, with a constitution granting a degree of internal autonomy. The Federation ceased to exist in 1901 when it was annexed to **New Zealand**, which was, at that time, a British self-governing colony. The authority of the Cook Islands expanded over time until 1965, when it became a self-governing state in free association with New Zealand. Since then, the head of state has been the monarch of New Zealand (who is actually the monarch of the **United Kingdom**), but all power belongs to the local government, which operates in accordance with the constitution and laws of the Cook Islands.

The majority of the population is Cook Islands Māori, who speak a language of the same name, related to the Tahitian and New Zealand Māori languages. On the islands of **Pukapuka** and **Nassau**, over 1,000 kilometres from Rarotonga, Pukapukan is spoken, a language related to those spoken on Samoa, Tuvalu, and other islands. Interestingly, today there are many more speakers of Cook Islands Māori and Pukapukan outside of the Cook Islands. It was actually the negative stance of the numerous diaspora that influenced the authorities of the Cook Islands not to implement their plan to change the country's name to something based on local culture and tradition. Instead, the Cook Islands Māori transliteration – Kūki 'Airani – is often seen added to the English name.

The Cook Islands currently use the New Zealand dollar, but from 1987 to 1995, they had their own currency, the Cook Islands dollar, which was the only currency with a triangular coin.

The main sources of income for the islands are tourism and pearl farming. Environmental protection is of great importance, as evidenced by the establishment of the 1,970,000-square-kilometre Marae Moana marine park, which covers the entire exclusive economic zone of the Cook Islands and represents the world's largest marine protected area.

KINGDOM OF **HUAHINE AND MAIAO**

Land of Queens and the pregnant woman

LOCATION: Polynesia, South Pacific Ocean
PERIOD: 18th century – 1895
AREA: 85 sq km
POPULATION: c. 3,000

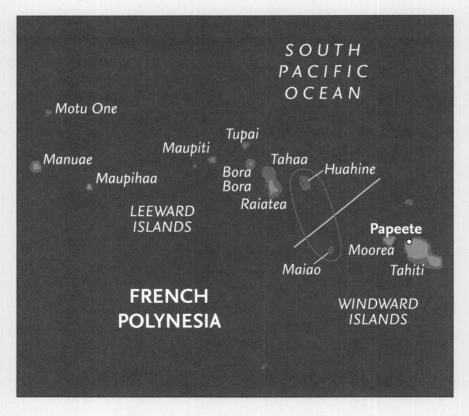

When, in the 9th century, Polynesian explorers first saw an island whose shape from a distance resembled a pregnant woman lying on her back, they named it Huahine, which according to one theory can be translated as 'pregnant woman'. For a long time, the island's inhabitants were divided into tribal communities, which were finally unified into a single kingdom in the 18th century, along with Maiao Island, which is 9 square kilometres in area and located about 100 kilometres to the south. This new kingdom was ruled by dynasties originating from Tahiti, whose royal house provided rulers for all the small surrounding kingdoms of that time. For example, the children of Queen Pomare IV of Tahiti became rulers of Tahiti, Bora Bora, and Raiatea-Tahaa.

When the famous Captain Cook visited Huahine in 1777, the Kingdom was led by Tehaapapa I, who ruled as sovereign from 1760 to 1790 with the title *ari'i rahi* ('great chief' or 'queen'). Rulers were often removed from power after internal conflicts or civil wars, as was the fate of Queen Teriitaria II, who lost her crown during one of these clashes. Although originally Queen of Tahiti, in 1815 she also became the formal Queen of Huahine and Maiao. During the first twenty years of her reign, she spent most of her time on Tahiti. She managed to prevent the French from occupying (or establishing a protectorate in) the small kingdoms of Bora Bora, Raiatea-Tahaa, and Huahine. Under pressure from **Britain**, she signed the Jarnac Convention in 1847, which recognised the independence of these island states.

During the rule of Queen Tehaapapa II (who reigned from 1868 to 1893), there were conflicts between pro- and anti-French groups. Towards the end of her reign, in 1890, she was forced to declare her land a French protectorate. Her son, Marama Teururai, was prime minister during his mother's final years of rule. After her death, he abdicated the throne in favour of his minor daughter, while still acting as regent. During this time, he and other leaders of Huahine surrendered power to the French Republic in 1895, thereby ending the Kingdom of Huahine and Maiao. The former regent became the mayor of Tefarerii village, a position he held until his death in 1909. Eight years later, his daughter Tehaapapa III, the last Queen of Huahine and Maiao, also died in the same village.

Today, Maiao and Huahine islands are part of the Society Islands, an archipelago within French Polynesia in the South Pacific. Since 2004, French Polynesia has been defined as a semi-autonomous overseas collectivity with the designation of Overseas Country of **France**.

Huahine consists of two islands connected by a bridge, situated in a shared lagoon. Despite the relatively small size of this combined island, it hosts a large number of *marae*, ancient open-air temples. It is possible that lush greenery and fertile valleys seemed enchanting to the ancient Polynesians, who believed such a paradise on Earth would facilitate easier contact with their gods.

REPUBLIC OF
KIRIBATI

Where the new day begins

LOCATION: Micronesia, central Pacific Ocean
PERIOD: since 1979
AREA: 717 sq km
POPULATION: 131,232

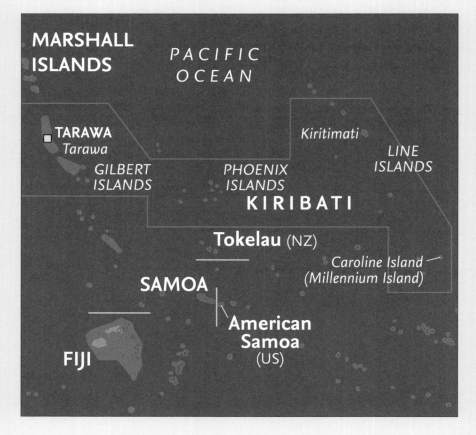

MARSHALL
ISLANDS

*PACIFIC
OCEAN*

TARAWA
Tarawa

Kiritimati

*LINE
ISLANDS*

*GILBERT
ISLANDS*

*PHOENIX
ISLANDS*

K I R I B A T I

Tokelau (NZ)

Caroline Island
(Millennium Island)

SAMOA

**American
Samoa**
(US)

FIJI

0   1,000 km

Most people would probably associate the Pacific islands with high numbers of tourists enjoying beaches with fine, white sand and crystal-clear waters. Unfortunately for Kiribati, though it does possess the sand and water, so far tourism has not developed as much as it could have.

Kiribati (pronounced Kiribass, meaning 'Gilbert' after the British captain Thomas Gilbert) is an extremely low-lying island republic located in the middle of the Pacific Ocean, at the intersection of the Equator and the 180th meridian. This makes it the only country in the world simultaneously in the northern, southern, eastern, and western hemispheres. When the **Gilbert Islands** archipelago gained independence from Britain in 1979 (calling itself the Republic of Kiribati), the United States decided to hand over its possessions, the Line Islands and Phoenix Islands archipelagos, to the new state. By merging these three groups of islands, the state of Kiribati was formed within its current borders. The problem with this union was that the International Date Line passed between the former British and American islands, so half of the country was in one day and the other half in another. Kiribati resolved the issue in 1995 by deciding to move the position of the Date Line around its territory, putting its Line Islands – the only place in the world – into the UTC+14 time zone. This is the earliest time zone of all, which means that these islands became the first to welcome each new day, as well as the New Year. This has been put to good use for tourism. There were also surrounding island states that occasionally 'jumped' into UTC+14, but it is a permanent time zone only in Kiribati. The uninhabited **Caroline Island**, closest to the Date Line, was renamed Millennium Island during the celebration to welcome in the New Year of 2000, with a billion viewers worldwide.

Today, Kiribati has just over 130,000 inhabitants, 90% of whom live on the Gilbert Islands. There is evidence that the first people settled on these islands several thousand years ago. Due to colonial rule, English is the official language of the Republic, but the second official language, Gilbertese or Kiribati, is used by over 95% of the population.

Kiribati covers a little over 700 square kilometres, but the islands are dispersed over 3.5 million square kilometres of ocean, which is approximately the combined area of India and Thailand. The westernmost point is the solitary island of Banaba, the highest island of Kiribati (81 metres) and formerly a major source of phosphate, whose legacy, now that the mining has ceased, is a landscape that resembles the surface of the moon. In the 1940s, the British decided to relocate almost the entire population of Banaba to the island of Rabi, 2,000 kilometres away and part of **Fiji**. Today, about 5,000 Banabans live on Rabi. They have autonomy within their new homeland but still officially govern their former island, which has about 300 inhabitants. The population of Rabi has dual citizenship of Fiji and Kiribati, so together with Banaba, they elect two representatives to the Kiribati parliament.

REPUBLIC OF THE
MARSHALL ISLANDS

The most watery nation,
with a nuclear past

LOCATION: Micronesia, central Pacific Ocean
PERIOD: since 1979
AREA: 181 sq km
POPULATION: 41,569

PACIFIC
OCEAN

Bikar

Enewetak   Bikini   Rongerik   Utirik
                        Rongelap   Taka
                                   Ailuk

Ujelang   Likiep
                      Ebadon   Roi-Namur   Wotje
              Ujae   Erikub
                      Lae   Kwajalein
                                           Maloelap
         MARSHALL   Namu   Aur
         ISLANDS   Arno
                        Ailinglapalap   Majuro
                                        MAJURO
                             Jaluit   Mili

     Kosrae
                        Ebon

Ralik

Ratak Chain

Chain

0   400 km

Roughly halfway between **Australia** and **Hawaii** there are two parallel chains of atolls, comprising over 1,000 islands of various sizes. The largest atoll among them is Kwajalein, whose 6 square kilometres of dry land surround an impressive lagoon of approximately 1,700 square kilometres. Together, the two chains of atolls make up the Marshall Islands, the most watery nation in the world. Due to the vast dispersion of small atolls and islands, this island nation controls territorial waters covering nearly 2 million square kilometres, which accounts for 98% of its combined land and sea area.

The Marshall Islands were first settled by Austronesian peoples around 4,000 years ago. Owing to them, the islands became suitable for human habitation as they introduced edible plants (such as coconuts and breadfruit) and animals (primarily domesticated chickens). The first Europeans, the Spaniards, visited the islands from the 16th century, but they were ultimately named in honour of Captain John Marshall, a British Pacific explorer from the late 18th century. A century later, German copra traders appeared, under whose influence the German Empire decided to colonise the archipelago in 1885. When **Japan** entered the First World War on the side of the Allies, it seized the opportunity to occupy small German possessions in the Pacific, including the Marshall Islands. In turn, Japan's alliance with **Germany** in the Second World War prompted the United States to seize the islands.

The end of the Second World War brought unprecedented displays of military power and destructive force for the Marshall Islands. From 1946 to 1958, the US detonated 67 nuclear bombs of various types on the Bikini and Enewetak atolls. Several smaller islands disappeared from the face of the Earth, and the majority of the native population was forced to relocate to other atolls. Runit Island on the Enewetak Atoll was chosen as the site for the disposal of a large amount of nuclear waste, and an enormous, concrete protective dome was built to cover it, known as the Runit Dome, Cactus Dome, or The Tomb, with a diameter of 115 metres. Today, there are concerns that the concrete may crack and release the stored waste into the ocean. On the other hand, numerous scientists point out that the land and sea around the dome are significantly more radioactive, so any potential leakage from Runit Dome would not pose a significant problem.

The United States recognised the Marshall Islands' constitution and president in 1979, and shortly afterwards the two nations signed a Compact of Free Association, whereby the US undertakes to protect the islands and provide various forms of financial assistance, along with the possibility of free migration and employment for citizens of the Marshall Islands in the US, and vice versa.

In 2011, the government of the Republic of the Marshall Islands took a significant step towards environmental protection in establishing the world's largest shark sanctuary, covering an area of almost 2 million square kilometres. This has meant a complete ban on shark fishing, intentional or unintentional, which will undoubtedly contribute to the recovery, and increase the numbers, of these magnificent marine predators.

The Runit Dome on Enewetak Atoll, Marshall Islands,
was constructed between 1977 and 1980 in order to contain
radioactive waste from America's Cold War nuclear tests.

The ruined ceremonial centre of Nan Modal in Pohnpei, Federated States of Micronesia, is under threat from the growth of mangroves in the waterways dividing the 100 islets on which it stands.

FEDERATED STATES OF MICRONESIA

*Islands of mystery –
rai stones and the bottom
of the world*

LOCATION: Micronesia, western Pacific Ocean
PERIOD: since 1979
AREA: 701 sq km
POPULATION: 114,164

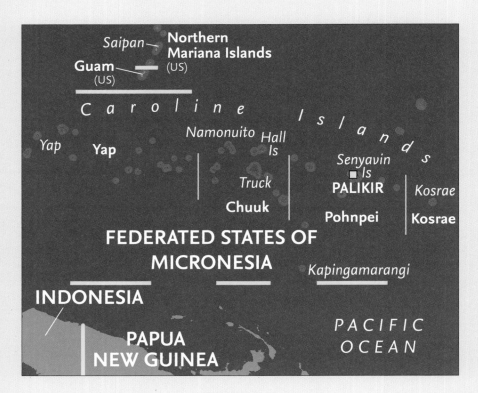

The Federated States of Micronesia (FSM) is yet another Pacific mini-island country, consisting of over 600 islands, occupying more than 700 square kilometres of land and covering around 3 million square kilometres of the ocean surface. The distance between its easternmost and westernmost points is an astonishing 2,700 kilometres. It is a federal state comprising four states, each represented by a star on the national flag: Yap, Chuuk, Pohnpei, and Kosrae. The first three constitute large archipelagos, while Kosrae consists of just one island. The state of Pohnpei also includes the remote atoll of Kapingamarangi, located only 130 kilometres north of the Equator. About 500 inhabitants of this isolated island speak a language from the Polynesian family, while the majority of FSM residents speak one of the Micronesian languages.

The first people settled on these archipelagos about 4,000 years ago. Over time, the small island tribal states were united under the leadership of the ruler of **Yap** island. Much later, so-called *rai* stones appeared on this island, unusual circular stone discs ranging from very small (a few centimetres in diameter) to enormous, at more than 3.5 metres in diameter, half a metre thick, and weighing around 4 tonnes. These stones were used in ceremonies, but it is believed they were also occasionally used as a form of currency. Interestingly, during these exchanges, the stone was not physically transferred; instead, it was simply announced to everyone that from that moment on, the rai had a new owner. One could say that the procedure resembles today's use of bank cards, without physical contact with money. Rai stones are also found on the license plates of Yap island.

Palikir, the capital of FSM, and Kolonia, the capital of the state of Pohnpei, are both on **Pohnpei** island. This island is one of the wettest places in the world, with over 7,600 millimetres of average annual rainfall in the mountainous areas. The eastern coast of Pohnpei island contains a true historical gem: the ancient city of Nan Madol, built partly on the natural island of Temwen and mostly on nearly 100 artificial islands linked by a network of channels. Most of the city is believed to have been built in the 12th and 13th centuries and was abandoned in the mid-17th century. It was constructed from natural basaltic stones, weighing from 5 to 50 tonnes.

Chuuk Lagoon, in the state of the same name, was the site of a major battle between the Americans and Japanese during the Second World War, when American forces sank about 50 Japanese ships. Today, this lagoon is a popular diving destination.

After the Second World War, FSM became a United Nations Trust Territory, and in 1979 its federated government came into effect.

Halfway between Yap island and the United States territory of **Guam**, in the depths of the Pacific, lies precisely that – the deepest measured point of the seabed, at a depth of nearly 11,000 metres and known as Challenger Deep. Only 27 people have descended to this point, in specialised submarines, a number similar to those who have been to the Moon (24), with one crucial difference: 12 astronauts have touched the surface of the Moon, whereas free-swimming in Challenger Deep's dark depths under enormous pressure remains an impossible mission for now.

REPUBLIC OF
NAURU

Island of bird gold

LOCATION: Micronesia, central Pacific Ocean
PERIOD: since 1968
AREA: 21 sq km
POPULATION: 12,668

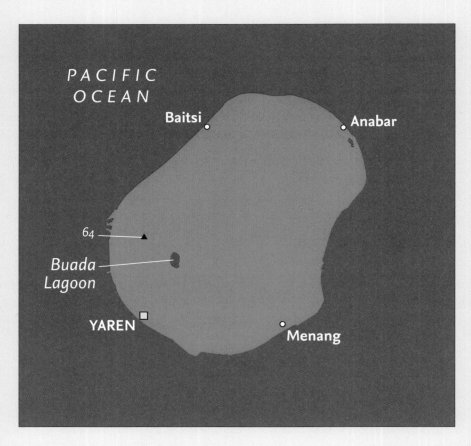

PACIFIC
OCEAN

Baitsi

Anabar

64

Buada
Lagoon

YAREN

Menang

0   2 km

At the beginning of the 20th century, huge deposits of guano were discovered on the then-German colony of Nauru (and the nearby island of Banaba, now part of Kiribati) and its exploitation soon began. Guano is seabirds' excrement, which has accumulated and dried on rocky land, producing a valuable ingredient for fertiliser, due to the high content of nitrogen, potassium and phosphate, which are essential nutrients for plant growth. Many such islands were colonised by greater powers to obtain the guano, and after the total exploitation of this resource, the native population was left with a landscape resembling a rocky desert or the surface of the moon.

At the start of the First World War, **Australia** took over Nauru from **Germany**, which was busy with the war in Europe, and the exploitation of the 'bird gold' continued unabated until the Second World War. Production declined during the war when German ships sank five Allied merchant ships near Nauru in 1940, and significantly damaged the phosphate production facilities on the island. This effective attack reduced the production of this precious substance, resulting in a decrease in agricultural production in Australia, New Zealand, and Japan.

After the war, the Australian authorities realised that living conditions on the island had significantly deteriorated due to mining activities, and so in 1964, they suggested that the population should relocate to Curtis Island off the coast of Queensland. However, no agreement was reached because the Nauruans did not want to become Australian citizens; instead, they sought independence for their new island, which Australia did not accept.

Two years after this proposal, in 1968, Nauru gained independence, and became the smallest republic in the world (the fact that the ring road, which surrounds the island, is less than 20 kilometres long is enough to understand its size). Two years later, the Nauru government bought and took over the phosphate production company, making the island's inhabitants among the richest people on the planet. At the same time, people began to eat extremely unhealthily, as fatty and sugary food arrived on the island, which had not been easily accessible before. Nauru is now considered to have the highest obesity rate in the world (according to some data, over 90% of the population).

As the government recognised that phosphate would not last forever, a large part of the revenue from this was transferred to a state fund. The purpose of the fund was to invest money worldwide so that it would be a source of finance when phosphate production came to an end. Unfortunately, the fund was poorly managed and so the money ran out. Meanwhile, the phosphate deposits dried up, tourism was not developed, and there is now very little fertile land on the island. From this perspective, the earlier proposal to relocate to Curtis Island may no longer seem so bad.

NIUE

The first Dark Sky Place

LOCATION: Polynesia, South Pacific Ocean
PERIOD: since 1974
AREA: 258 sq km
POPULATION: 1,934

SOUTH
PACIFIC
OCEAN

Mutalau

Makefu

ALOFI

Hakupu

0   10 km

In 1774, Captain James Cook wanted to be the first European to land on the island of Niue, but he was unsuccessful, as the existing inhabitants didn't let him come on shore. These inhabitants were descendants of settlers from **Samoa** and **Tonga**, who arrived on Niue in the early 10th century and the 16th century respectively. In the early 19th century, British missionaries arrived on Niue, and by the end of that century, local chiefs and rulers sought protection for their island from **Britain**, fearing that other colonial powers would simply occupy the island. The first request was denied, but upon repeated pleas, Niue officially became a British protectorate. However, by 1901, the British had transferred jurisdiction of the island to **New Zealand**, a situation that remained until 1974. That year, a new constitution was adopted in Niue, and citizens voted in a referendum to have a self-governing state in free association with New Zealand. The monarch of New Zealand (and Britain) therefore became the ruler of this small island, and political life proceeded without the presence of political parties, although there was one party for some time. Today, each of the 14 villages elects one member to the state parliament, with an additional six members elected by the entire island. New Zealand is in charge of the defence and diplomacy of its small ally. Recently, however, Niue has been taking more control over its relations with other countries, often not entirely in line with New Zealand's foreign policy.

Most of Niue's population speaks Niuean, a language closely related to Tongan. English is widely spoken, due to the close ties with New Zealand that have existed for over 120 years.

With an area just under 260 square kilometres, Niue is probably the largest coral island in the world, surrounded by coral reef on all sides, except for a small passage near the capital, Alofi.

The main sources of income for the small island state are agriculture (vanilla is one of the main products), fishing (mostly various types of tuna), and tourism (swimming, diving, hiking through dense forests and plantations in the island's interior, whale watching, and exploration of numerous caves, some of which are underwater). Niue also offers something unique to its visitors: in 2020, the entire island was declared the world's first Dark Sky Place. This means that throughout the island, lighting meets several strict rules of the International Dark-Sky Association (IDA). Light should only be used if necessary, where necessary, and when necessary, and should be as dim and warm as possible. Interested tourists are offered night tours, during which it is possible to see significantly more stars than in large cities.

The official currency of Niue is the New Zealand dollar, but unique collector coins are occasionally issued, which can formally be used as a means of payment on the island (although the nominal value is usually much lower than the selling value). These coins feature characters from Star Wars, Superman, Spiderman, Harry Potter, Batman, Pokémon, as well as historical figures such as Salvador Dali, Alexander the Great, and Genghis Khan, and are a fun way to make some extra dollars.

KINGDOM OF **RAPA NUI**

Easter Island for the Europeans

LOCATION: Southeastern Pacific Ocean

PERIOD: up to 1902

AREA: 163 sq km

POPULATION: c. 2,000

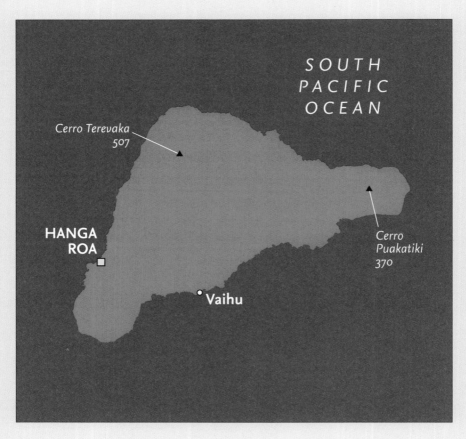

SOUTH
PACIFIC
OCEAN

Cerro Terevaka
507

HANGA
ROA

Cerro
Puakatiki
370

Vaihu

0   5 km

Fascinating sculptures, known as *moai*, and the ancient Rongorongo script are the first associations of many with Rapa Nui (Easter Island – known in Spanish as Isla de Pascua), an isolated island located 3,500 kilometres off the Pacific coast of **South America**. Rapa Nui (Easter Island) is likely to have been the furthest point of the incredible spread of Austronesian peoples from **Taiwan** – westward to Madagascar, southward to New Zealand, and eastward to Easter Island. It is still unknown when the ancestors of today's Rapa Nui population (who refer to themselves and their language by the same name) arrived on the island, but there are three possibilities: the 4th century, the 8th century, or perhaps as recently as the 13th century. They brought bananas, sugarcane, chickens, and rats, and developed an organised society under the absolute rule of kings (*ariki*), surrounded by priests and warriors.

The first Europeans arrived on the island in the first half of the 18th century, one Easter Sunday (hence the European name of the island), estimating a population of over 2,000 people at that time. In the 1860s, Peruvian enslavers reached Easter Island and took around 1,500 people for forced labour. After a few years, the Peruvian government reluctantly banned enslavement, but the Rapa Nui who managed to return brought back numerous diseases that claimed many lives.

Jean-Baptiste Dutrou-Bornier, a French sailor with a dubious past, decided to settle on the island in 1868 and establish a large sheep ranch. He soon married a local woman named Koreto, from the royal family, in order to declare himself King. At the same time, he proposed to **France** that Rapa Nui be declared its protectorate, which was not accepted. He ruled despotically as the number of his subjects rapidly decreased, leaving just over 100 by 1877. Around that time, the King died, although the circumstances of his death remain unclear.

The Tahitian prince Alexander Ariipaea Salmon became the new landowner on the island. Although he did not assume any title for himself, he still effectively governed Rapa Nui. He was remembered as a benevolent ruler who encouraged islanders to produce artistic items and participate in island governance. Following the suggestion of a powerful bishop from Tahiti and local missionaries, a new king of the island, Atamu Tekena, was elected in 1883, although with little real political power. In 1888, the King signed a treaty of protectorate (interpreted as such by Rapa Nui) or cession to **Chile** (interpreted as such by Chile). King Atamu died in 1892, and Riro Kainga was chosen as the new ruler.

At that time, a civil war erupted in Chile, preventing the takeover of Rapa Nui. This was a period when the new King managed to establish relative peace and stability for his compatriots. However, immediately after the war ended, Chileans returned to Easter Island and imposed harsh conditions once again. In 1899, the King went to Chile to negotiate with the government to improve the situation but died under unclear circumstances. Although two more kings led the island after him (until 1902), Riro Kainga is considered the last king of the small island in the blue expanses of the South Pacific.

KINGDOM OF **RURUTU**

Two minor monarchs standing together

LOCATION: Polynesia, South Pacific Ocean
PERIOD: early 1800s–1900
AREA: 33 sq km
POPULATION: c. 1,000

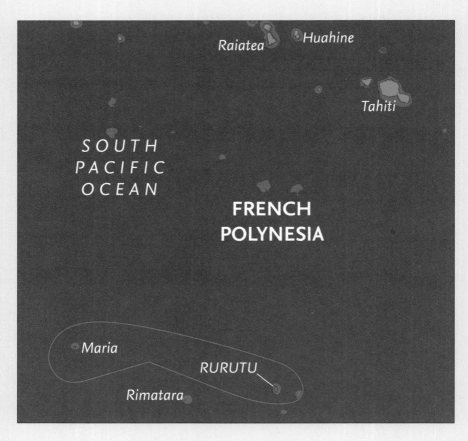

Raiatea Huahine

Tahiti

SOUTH
PACIFIC
OCEAN

**FRENCH
POLYNESIA**

Maria

RURUTU

Rimatara

0   200 km

French expansion in the South Pacific region led to the imposition of a protectorate on the most powerful local kingdom, Tahiti, in 1842. Formal annexation and transformation into a colony took place in 1880, however, some smaller regional kingdoms managed in various ways to survive more or less independently for several more decades. One such state was the Kingdom of Rurutu on the island of the same name.

Rurutu Island occupies the northern part of the Tubuai Islands (known in French as Îles Australes) within today's French Polynesia. The island has an area of 33 square kilometres, is covered with dense forest, and the highest peak is almost 390 metres. The first Polynesians are believed to have arrived during the 10th century. Although the name of the island can be translated as 'together (*ruru*) we always stand (*tu*)', the first unified royal authority over the entire island was only formed at the beginning of the 19th century by Teramana Teuruarii I, who ruled until 1822. As the King had no offspring, he adopted a member of the local aristocracy from the island of Huahine, thus continuing the independent rule of the small Kingdom.

When King Paa Teuruarii III abdicated in 1886 to return to Huahine, the island of his ancestors, he was succeeded by his minor son Epatiana Teuruarii IV (his sister was the mother of Tehaapapa III, the last ruler of the Kingdom of Huahine and Maiao). Until the young king came of age, the country was ruled by his mother, Queen Taarouru, as regent. Together, the two made the decision to abolish the death penalty and banish convicted criminals to the remote atoll of Îles Maria (Polynesian name: Nororotu). At the same time, a Protestant church was built in Moerai, Rurutu's main settlement.

By this time **France** had already conquered Tahiti and almost all the surrounding islands. Towards the end of the 19th century, only the kingdoms of Rurutu and neighbouring friendly Rimatara (10 square kilometres, c. 550 inhabitants), led by the minor monarchs King Teuruarii IV and Queen Tamaeva IV, retained their independence. As the rulers were more sympathetic to predominantly Protestant Britain than to Catholic France, in 1888, they visited the Kingdom of Rarotonga (today the main island of the Cook Islands), from where they sent a request to Queen Victoria, asking that the **United Kingdom** place them under its protection. The request was rejected, but it was a signal to the French to act quickly: Rurutu was declared a French protectorate on 27 March 1889, and Rimatara two days later (historians disagree on whether these protectorates were voluntary or imposed). Both Kingdoms added the French tricolor to the upper left corner of their flags, as a protectorate symbol.

The internal arrangement of the Rurutu Kingdom was not significantly changed during this period. The island was still ruled by the King, chiefs and local judges until 1900, when Rurutu was officially annexed to French Polynesia. The former King received a pension and was appointed head of the former capital of Moerai. A number of descendants of Teuruarii IV have retained positions of influence on the island over the years – a son held the position of chief of Moerai for a time, a grandson was mayor of Rurutu in the 1970s, and a great-grandson has the unofficial name of Teuruarii VII.

*A carving of Tangaroa, the Polynesian god of the sea.
On Rurutu he symbolises the island's connection to water
and is honoured as the creator of oceans and marine life.*

Nukunonu and Motuhaga, the two main settlements on Nukunonu Atoll, are connected by a concrete bridge at the point where the ocean and the lagoon meet. The whole of Tokelau is a low-lying territory, threatened by cyclones, rising sea levels and climate change.

TOKELAU

Four-star flag for three atolls

LOCATION: Polynesia, South Pacific Ocean
PERIOD: New Zealand dependency since 1949
AREA: 10 sq km
POPULATION: 1,871

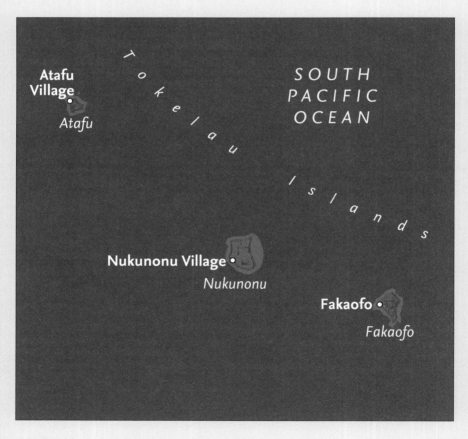

Atafu
Village
Atafu

Tokelau Islands

SOUTH
PACIFIC
OCEAN

Nukunonu Village
Nukunonu

Fakaofo
Fakaofo

0   50 km

This tiny territory consists of three atolls located in the South Pacific, halfway between **New Zealand** and **Hawaii**. Tokelau is a dependent territory of New Zealand and not a sovereign state.

Polynesians first inhabited these atolls around 1,000 years ago, and for a long time, each atoll was its own state, with varying relationships with its two neighbouring atolls. These relationships between the atolls remained unchanged even with the coming of the first Europeans, until in 1863, Peruvian enslavers raided the atolls, enslaving nearly all able-bodied men. A few years later, **Britain** unilaterally declared the islands its protectorate, and in 1899, at the request of the local authorities, they were annexed to the British Empire. Later, Tokelau was transferred to the jurisdiction of New Zealand, becoming an integral part in 1949.

Today, Tokelau largely operates as a semi-autonomous territory, with a governance system based on traditional methods for managing these remote atolls. Each atoll has its leader (*faipule*), and each serves one year as head of state (*Ulu-o-Tokelau*). There are no political parties, and the parliament (General Fono) consists of all three atoll leaders, the mayors (*pulenuku*) of the three largest villages, representatives of village elders, and male and female representatives. The government consists of these leaders and mayors, who also hold roles in assigned ministries. New Zealand laws do not directly apply to Tokelau unless approved by local authorities. Defence remains the responsibility of New Zealand, but customs and a dozen police officers are under Tokelau's independent control.

Since 2005, two referendums have been held, in which citizens could choose if they wanted to become a sovereign state in free association with New Zealand. Despite being listed by the United Nations as a non-self-governing territory, both times the majority voted against a change in status. Interestingly, on both occasions, a simple majority favoured self-governance, but the necessary two-thirds majority was not achieved (the 2007 referendum missed this by only 16 votes). This decision was likely influenced by the Tokelauan diaspora in New Zealand, where five times more Tokelauans reside than on Tokelau itself, and the $10 million in annual financial aid received from the New Zealand government.

The proposed Tokelau flag from 2007 featured four stars representing the three Tokelau atolls and Swains Island (known in Tokelauan as Olohega and known in Samoan as Olosega) which belongs to the **United States** but which Tokelau has claimed for decades, despite being 200 kilometres away. The US and New Zealand disagree with this claim and consider that Swains Island (now uninhabited) belongs to **American Samoa**. The flag proposal was modified, and in 2009, a new flag featuring four stars arranged in the Southern Cross constellation was adopted.

KINGDOM OF
TONGA

An empire of noble descent

LOCATION: Polynesia, South Pacific Ocean
PERIOD: since at least the 12th century
AREA: 748 sq km
POPULATION: c. 106,858

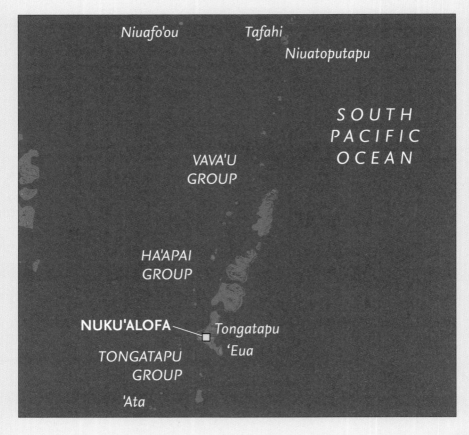

Niuafo'ou   Tafahi
Niuatoputapu

SOUTH
PACIFIC
OCEAN

VAVA'U
GROUP

HA'APAI
GROUP

NUKU'ALOFA — Tongatapu
'Eua
TONGATAPU
GROUP
'Ata

0   250 km

Several monarchies in Oceania, including **Australia** and **New Zealand**, are headed by the British sovereign, but only Tonga has been ruled by native dynasties for centuries. The current King, Tupou VI, belongs to the Tupou dynasty, which has ruled uninterrupted since 1845.

Historical findings indicate that ancient Melanesians settled on Tongatapu, one of the Tongan islands, as early as the 9th century. A new culture and identity began to form there, eventually giving rise to the Polynesians as a distinct people. By the 12th century, Tongan kings had extended their authority throughout the South Pacific, from New Caledonia in the west to certain islands of French Polynesia in the eastern ocean, creating a powerful Tongan Empire.

The first Europeans to see Tonga were the Dutch in the early 17th century, and by the late 18th century, the first Christian missionaries from **Britain** arrived, quickly spreading Protestantism among the local population. George Tupou I became King of Tonga in 1845, and exactly 30 years later, he introduced a liberal constitution (for that time), ensuring freedom of the press and limiting the power of chiefs. The constitution also defined a flag, which had been used informally before, making it one of the oldest national flags still in use.

Out of fear of the German ships that were increasingly navigating the waters around Tonga, King George Tupou II signed a treaty in 1900, making it a protectorate of Britain, which had partial control over foreign policy and finances. However, Tonga never renounced its sovereignty or its indigenous monarchy, which distinguished it from all other islands and states in Oceania. Exactly 70 years later, in 1970, the protection treaty expired, and Tonga fully assumed its independence. In the early 21st century, Tongan kings began democratising their country, giving significant powers to the prime minister (at that time, the first prime minister who was not of noble descent was elected).

Tonga is a largely religious society, and the lives of the entire population are greatly influenced by both Polynesian traditions and Christianity. The majority, over 70%, live on the main island of Tongatapu, which serves as the centre of politics, culture, and the monarchy. As this island has been the centre of various Tongan states for centuries, it is no surprise that today it is home to the capital, Nuku'alofa, as well as three former capitals. In the former capital, Mu'a, there are over 20 royal tombs, as this city was the centre of the Tongan Empire for almost 400 years.

Tonga's economy mainly relies on agriculture – including the cultivation of bananas, coconuts, vanilla, and sweet potatoes – and fishing. Tourism is still underdeveloped, although Tonga has beautiful nature and a rich history to offer the visitor. Another source of income is the trade in unusual postage stamps, with bold colours and unique designs, and often in unexpected shapes – bananas, the island of Tongatapu, gold coins, or hearts – which are a real treat for philatelists worldwide.

TUVALU

Cave men and television income

LOCATION: Polynesia, South Pacific Ocean
PERIOD: since 1978
AREA: 25 sq km
POPULATION: 11,312

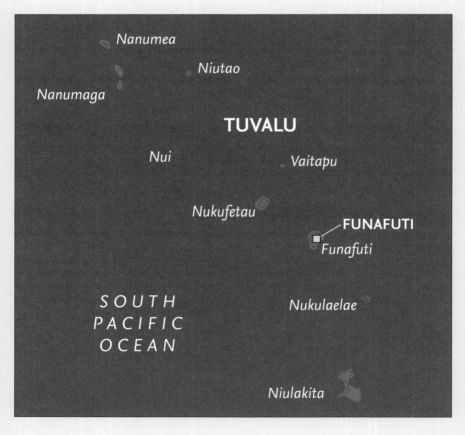

Nanumea

Niutao

Nanumaga

TUVALU

Nui

Vaitapu

Nukufetau

FUNAFUTI
Funafuti

*SOUTH
PACIFIC
OCEAN*

Nukulaelae

Niulakita

0   200 km

Tuvalu is one of the smallest independent countries today, both in terms of population and land area, and also one of the least-visited tourist destinations. This microstate is a group of about ten atolls and islands located in west Polynesia. The name of this island group can be translated as 'eight (islands) together' because ancient Polynesians originally settled on eight out of the nine islands. In more recent history, the Spaniards were the first Europeans to sight the Tuvalu islands in 1568. Centuries later, in 1861, an ocean storm brought a British missionary from the Cook Islands, initiating the spread of Christianity among Tuvalu's inhabitants (98% of today's population belongs to various Christian denominations). Only two years later, Peruvian enslavers took many able-bodied locals for forced labour in **Peru**.

At the end of the 19th century, Tuvalu became a British protectorate, initially as part of the Gilbert and Ellice Islands protectorate, and from 1916, as part of the eponymic colony. During the Second World War, it served as a strategic Allied base for further Pacific battles. Following a referendum in 1974, the colony of Gilbert and Ellice Islands split into two separate entities. Ellice Islands gained independence in 1978, under the name Tuvalu, while the Gilbert Islands became the Republic of Kiribati in 1979.

Tuvalu has very little land area, much of which is of poor quality and frequently flooded by seawater. Funafuti, the main atoll and capital, is a narrow strip of land 2.5 square kilometres in area, and 20 to 400 metres wide, surrounding a large lagoon of about 275 square kilometres. Fogafale (also known as Fongafale), the largest island within Funafuti Atoll, is home to the parliament, government offices, national bank, police, court, hospital, and airport, as well as 6,000 people.

The British monarch is the head of state with the title King of Tuvalu, represented on the island by a governor-general. The islanders had the opportunity in two referendums (1986 and 2008) to declare whether they wanted their small country to become a republic – both times the response was negative. English and Tuvaluan are the national languages, but all official functions of the parliament and other government bodies are conducted in Tuvaluan. However, even such a small country can have its ethnic and linguistic minorities, and on the Nui atoll, residents speak either Gilbertese (Kiribati) or Tuvaluan, depending on their ancestral origins.

Tourism is hindered by Tuvalu's remoteness. The primary economic activities include fishing, and the sale of postage stamps and the .tv internet domain, which is a popular choice for television-related websites and organisations.

Off the coast of one of Tuvalu's northernmost islands, Nanumaga (also known as Nanumanga), at a depth of around 40 metres, lies an underwater cave that supposedly contains evidence of human habitation dating back about 8,000 years (smoke residues on the walls and burnt corals). However, scientific evidence suggests that the first Austronesians arrived in the region around 3,000 years ago. The cave was discovered based on a local legend describing a large house under the sea. Did ancient people truly live in this cave before the sea level rose or was the evidence misinterpreted (intentionally or accidentally)?

OTHER 'SMALL COUNTRIES'

*The Principality of Sealand is one of the longest-existing micronations.
It is based on HM Fort Roughs, an offshore platform in the North Sea,
12 kilometres off the coast of East Anglia, England.*

COCOS (KEELING) ISLANDS

Cocos (Keeling) Islands is an Australian External Territory located in the Indian Ocean, halfway between **Australia** and **India**. It consists of nearly 30 islands grouped into two atolls with a total area of 14 square kilometres. Only two of these islands, both in the South Keeling atoll, are inhabited. The village of Bantam is located on Home Island and has 450 residents, mostly of Malay descent. The capital of the territory is West Island, with just under 150 residents, mostly of European descent, making it one of the smallest capitals in the world. Despite its small size, the town features administrative buildings, an airport, a hotel, and a shop.

The whole territory has fewer than 600 inhabitants, the majority of whom are of Malay descent. As a result, this area is the only part of Australia where the majority of the population (about two thirds) identifies as Muslim, with a similar proportion speaking Cocos Islands Malay. The Shire of Cocos (Keeling) Islands represents the partially self-governing local government of this external territory.

The islands were once a British colony which, from the 19th century, belonged to the Clunies-Ross family as a copra plantation. Most residents are descendants of Malay workers from that plantation. The **United Kingdom** transferred the islands to Australia in 1955, but it was not until 1979 that land was purchased from the Clunies-Ross family and the current territory was established.

JERVIS BAY TERRITORY

When listing Australian states and territories, one territory is often overlooked. With its 68 square kilometres and only 350 residents, Jervis Bay Territory (JBT) is not easily noticeable on maps of **Australia**, which itself covers nearly 7,700,000 square kilometres.

This small territory was established in 1915 when the federal government decided that Canberra, Australia's capital city, should have a port and access to the sea. New South Wales agreed to cede its 68 square kilometres of peninsula south of Jervis Bay. JBT has often been considered part of the Australian Capital Territory (ACT), but it never officially was. It is part of the electoral division of Fenner, which consists mostly of

Canberra's northern suburbs. While almost all ACT laws apply in JBT, and the Australian Federal Police are responsible for law enforcement in both territories, local services such as refuse collection are provided by surrounding towns in New South Wales.

Most of JBT's land is owned by the Wreck Bay Aboriginal Community, which includes the villages of Wreck Bay and the vast Booderee National Park, home to the only botanic garden owned by First Australians. Booderee means 'bay of plenty (of fish)' in the nearly extinct Dhurga language. The northern part of the peninsula hosts the Royal Australian Navy's training facility and Jervis Bay Village. Nearby Bowen Island, also part of JBT, is home to about 10,000 Australian Little Penguins.

PITCAIRN ISLANDS

There are not many political territories whose population count is close to the number of letters in their official name. One such example is the United Kingdom Overseas Territory of Pitcairn, Henderson, Ducie and Oeno Islands, with fewer than 50 permanent residents. This is the last remaining British territory in the Pacific, consisting of four volcanic islands with a total area of 43 square kilometres, located approximately halfway between **Australia** and **Peru**. Only Pitcairn Island is inhabited, so the entire archipelago is usually referred to as the Pitcairn Islands. Although Polynesians were known to have settled on these islands centuries ago, they had been uninhabited for a long period by the time Europeans first sighted them in the early 17th century.

The first European settlement was established by mutineers from HMS *Bounty*, who arrived on the island in 1790 with a group of Tahitians. After initial conflicts which resulted in the deaths of many mutineers and Tahitians, a period of peaceful coexistence among the remaining newcomers began. The isolation of the island led to the development of a new language known as Pitkern, a blend of 18th-century English and Tahitian. Today, all inhabitants of Pitcairn Island (Pitkern Ailen in Pitkern language) typically speak this language, and both Pitkern and English are taught equally in the island's only school located in its only town, Adamstown.

The entire exclusive economic zone of the archipelago has been declared a marine protected area since 2015, effectively giving the 50 residents of Pitcairn Island some form of control over the impressive marine area of 850,000 square kilometres.

The least densely populated territories

FALKLAND ISLANDS

The Falkland Islands are an archipelago in the South Atlantic, situated approximately 500 kilometres off the coast of **South America**. Politically, the islands are a United Kingdom Overseas Territory, claimed by Argentina for decades under its own name, Islas Malvinas. The dispute arises from uncertainty over who first sighted and/or colonised the islands. The problem escalated in 1982 when **Argentina** launched a military invasion of the islands. After initial Argentine success, a four-month war followed, resulting in victory for the **United Kingdom** and the restoration of British control over the Falkland Islands.

However, the defeat in the war did not prevent almost every subsequent Argentinian government from requesting the return of the archipelago from the United Kingdom. A referendum conducted in 2013 on the Falkland Islands showed that almost all voters wished for their islands to remain a United Kingdom Overseas Territory.

Today, the islands, with an area of 12,170 square kilometres, are home to 3,780 inhabitants, resulting in a population density of only 0.31 people per square kilometre. For comparison, **Qatar** has a similar area (11,580 square kilometres) but significantly more inhabitants (2,800,000), making its population density nearly 600 times greater.

The wildlife of the Falklands is unique: there are no native amphibians, reptiles, or trees. The only terrestrial mammal documented during the European colonisation of the islands was the warrah, a somewhat mysterious, tame, and curious animal from the dog species, which colonists quickly exterminated, both to protect their sheep and for its high-quality fur.

GORNO-BADAKHSHAN AUTONOMOUS REGION

The Gorno-Badakhshan Autonomous Region, the official English translation of the Russian name, is a region in eastern **Tajikistan**, which is situated between **Afghanistan** and **China**. Looking at the administrative map of the Republic of Tajikistan, the Gorno-Badakhshan Autonomous Region (abbreviated as GBAO) occupies 45% of Tajikistan's territory. However, the 227,000 inhabitants of GBAO constitute just a little over 2% of Tajikistan's total population. The ratio of population to area in this autonomous region (64,200 square kilometres) makes GBAO one of the most sparsely populated territories in the world (3.54 people per square kilometre).

Historically, the region of Badakhshan also includes parts of northeastern Afghanistan (Badakhshan Province) and one of the westernmost parts of China (Tashkurgan Tajik Autonomous County). The Tajik part of this region was reduced by about 1,000 square kilometres in 2011 when the parliament approved ceding that portion of mountainous land to the People's Republic of China. This resolution settled a 130-year-long border dispute, during which China had previously claimed as much as 28,000 square kilometres, or 40%, of GBAO's territory.

The majority of the population consists of Pamiris, a group of various Eastern Iranian ethnic people who speak different, often mutually unintelligible, languages. A smaller percentage of the population speaks Kyrgyz and Tajik as their native languages, while many use Russian as a lingua franca among communities.

GREENLAND

The **Kingdom of Denmark**, or Danish Realm, consists of Denmark proper and two autonomous regions: the Faroe Islands and Greenland.

Greenland, or Kalaallit Nunaat ('Land of the Kalaallit'), is located in North America and at approximately 2,175,600 square kilometres, it is the largest island in the world. Around 56,466 people live in this vast area (roughly equivalent to the combined area of **France**, **Germany**, **Italy**, **Spain**, and **Sweden**), resulting in a population density of only 0.03 people per square kilometre. Most of the population is concentrated along the southwest coast, where the capital Nuuk is located, the largest city in Greenland with around 20,000 inhabitants. On the other hand, the largest part of the island's surface (75%) is completely uninhabited for a simple reason: it is covered with permanent ice, with a thickness reaching up to three kilometres. Interestingly, the warmest parts of Greenland, in the far south, are sparsely populated.

The majority of Greenland's population are Inuit, making this autonomous territory the only region in the Americas with an indigenous majority. The official language is Greenlandic, which has three dialects (some consider them separate languages): West Greenlandic or Kalaallisut (spoken by 50,000 people), East Greenlandic or Tunumiisut (3,000 speakers), and Polar Inuit or Inuktun (1,000 speakers in the north). Of course, Danish is also still widely used.

In terms of transportation, Greenland is unusual: there are no railways or roads between settlements, so transportation is mainly by ship, plane, or snowmobile.

MONGOLIA

The Mongol Empire of the 13th and 14th centuries encompassed large parts of Asia and Eastern Europe, with an area of 24 million square kilometres, making it the largest contiguous empire in history. Mongolia today is considerably smaller, but with an area of 1,565,000 square kilometres, it is ranked the 18th-largest country in the world by land area. However, its small population (3,398,366) results in a population density of around 2.17 people per square kilometre, making it the absolute leader in terms of the world's most sparsely populated sovereign state which is still in existence.

Three quarters of Mongolia's population lives in the capital, Ulan Bator, and surrounding smaller cities, while one quarter inhabits the vast steppes (dry, grassy plains) in the country's interior. The high mountains have a harsh climate and the extremely inhospitable Gobi Desert along the border with **China** (Mongolia shares borders only with the People's Republic of China and Russia) is almost uninhabited. Ethnic Mongols comprise about 95% of the population, with the other 5% of citizens mainly belonging to Turkic peoples, such as Kazakhs and Tuvans. The official language is Mongolian, which has several dialects. Cyrillic and traditional Mongolian script are used for writing.

The southern parts of Mongolia are home to the wild Bactrian camel, the only truly wild species of camel and related animals in the Old World, as well as the Przewalski's horse, the only completely wild species of horse that has never been successfully domesticated.

NAMIBIA

With its 824,292 square kilometres, Namibia truly lives up to its name. The country is named after the Namib, a vast coastal desert that stretches along Namibia's entire Atlantic coastline (and extends partially into neighbouring **Angola** and **South Africa**). The word *Namib* itself derives from the Khoekhoe language of the Nama people, known for its use of clicks, and it means 'vast place'. However, the number of people inhabiting this vast area is actually quite small.

Today, Namibia has 2,567,012 inhabitants, resulting in a population density of about 3.11 people per square kilometre. This places Namibia among the most sparsely populated sovereign countries in the world, alongside **Mongolia** and **Australia**. The largest ethnic groups trace their origins to the Bantu peoples who arrived in present-day Namibia in the 14th century. The largest of these peoples, the Ovambo, now constitute about half of Namibia's population. Thousands of years before the Bantu, the area was inhabited by numerous indigenous peoples such as the San and the Nama (Namaqua), who today comprise about 1% and 4% of Namibia's population respectively.

Apart from its relatively sparse population, Namibia is a country of incredible nature. It is home to Dune 7, one of the tallest sand dunes in the world (over 380 metres), the Namib Desert, likely the oldest desert on Earth, the Skeleton Coast, known for its numerous shipwrecks and frequent fog (referred to by the San people as 'The Land God Made in Anger'), and one of Africa's largest national parks, Etosha National Park.

SVALBARD

Svalbard is a Norwegian archipelago in the Arctic Ocean, situated almost halfway between the northern coast of **Norway** and the **North Pole**. It covers an area of just over 61,000 square kilometres and is home to 2,500 inhabitants (population density: 0.04 people per square kilometre), nearly 40% of whom are not Norwegians but Russians, Ukrainians, Poles, Germans, and Thais.

The uniqueness of Svalbard lies in the Svalbard Treaty, signed in Paris in 1920 and effective from 1925. The nature of this treaty is that it recognises Norwegian sovereignty over this icy archipelago, while allowing all other nations the right to fish and extract minerals found on the islands. **Russia** (and prior to that, the Soviet Union) has been utilising this opportunity for decades. The Russian consulate, probably the northernmost diplomatic mission in the world, is located in Barentsburg. No visa is required for anyone to live and work on Svalbard, regardless of the duration or purpose of their stay. The archipelago is not part of the Schengen Zone or the European Economic Area, even though Norway is a member of both organisations. Similarly, Svalbard is not part of any Norwegian province, but is under Norwegian sovereignty.

Five kilometres from Longyearbyen, the archipelago's administrative centre, lies the Svalbard Global Seed Vault, a well-secured facility where a vast collection of seeds from various plants is stored. Its purpose is to safeguard the diversity of the world's plant species in the event of any kind of disaster.

Micronations

Although people might think that the terms 'microstate' and 'micronation' are synonymous, this is by no means correct. Microstates are (more or less) internationally recognised states of a small size and/or population. They possess (almost) all the usual characteristics of states: defined territory, government, economic and political relations with other states. As for micronations, the *Collins English Dictionary* defines them as 'an entity, typically existing only on the internet or within the private property of its members, that lays claim to sovereign status as an independent nation, but which is unrecognized by real nations'. There are numerous reasons why someone might decide to create a micronation: political protest, social experiment, joke, satire, expression of a personal stance. Official states, regardless of size, almost never react to the declaration of an independent micronation. There are a great number of micronations; they appear quickly and usually disappear even faster. Here are a few examples:

Principality of Sealand – one of longest-existing self-proclaimed micronations. It is based on HM Fort Roughs, an offshore platform in the North Sea, 12 kilometres off the coast of Essex in **England**. It was founded in 1967 by Patrick 'Paddy' Roy Bates, former major of the British Army, whose son Michael Roy Bates is current Prince of Sealand. Sealand has a constitution, flag and passport, and occupies an area of several hundred square metres. In 1987, the **United Kindgom** extended its territorial waters to 22 kilometres, which brought Sealand into British territorial waters.

Republic of Saugeais – a micronation that emerged in 1947 as a joke between a local politician and a hotel owner in the town of Montbenoît, **France**, on the border with **Switzerland**. Allegedly, the hotelier jokingly asked his guest for a passport to enter the 'Republic of Saugeais', upon which the politician jokingly declared the hotel owner as the president of the new free republic. This title later passed to the hotelier's widow, who took her state to a higher level by printing money and passports. The president's daughter succeeded her mother after her death in 2006, and in 2022, the former prime minister of the Republic, Simon Marguet, became the new president.

Principality of Seborga – a micronation encompassing the town of Seborga in northwestern **Italy**, near the border with **France**, declared independence in 1963. The citizens elected a prince, formed a government, and designed a flag and currency, which is still occasionally used alongside the euro. The state motto was in Latin: *Sub Umbra Sedi*, which translates to 'I sat in the shade'. The basis for its independence is an alleged historical document claiming that Seborga was not legitimately included in the newly formed Kingdom of Italy in 1861.

Republic of Rose Island – a micronation that Italian Giorgio Rosa declared on an artificial platform in the **Adriatic Sea** in 1968. The platform was located about ten kilometres from the city of Rimini, supposedly outside Italian territorial waters. The official language of this micronation was Esperanto, postage stamps were printed, and allegedly a separate currency and flag were designed. The Italian government viewed President Rosa's idea as a way to profit from tourists without paying taxes. Less than two months after declaring independence, Italian police seized the platform. After several unsuccessful attempts to bomb the platform, it was finally toppled by a severe storm in late February 1969.

Sultanate of M'Simbati – a micronation formed in 1959 on the southernmost coast of the then British colony of Tanganyika. Englishman Latham Leslie Moore purchased the M'Simbati Peninsula near the town of Mtwara. He soon declared the independence of his sultanate and designed a new flag. After the unification of Tanganyika and Zanzibar to form **Tanzania**, Moore sought recognition of independence from the President of Tanzania and the United Nations, but received no response.

Republic of Parva Domus Magna Quies – a micronation whose Latin name means 'small house, big rest' was formed in 1878 in an elegant villa in Montevideo, the capital of **Uruguay**, across from the famous Parque de las Instrucciones del Año XIII. The constitution of this micronation admits a maximum of 250 citizens at any time, all exclusively male. Every year, on Uruguay's national holiday, the 'borders' of Parva Domus are open to visitors who wish to see the national museum, garden, and theatre.

Republic of Minerva – a micronation was formed on Minerva Reefs, a submerged atoll in the Pacific between **Fiji** and **Tonga**. Las Vegas millionaire real estate agent, Michael Oliver, had an idea for a libertarian society here, free from taxes, welfare and subsidies, and the island would survive predominantly on tourism and fishing. In 1972, construction began on the artificial island on the reef. Surrounding island nations (Fiji, **Samoa** (then called Western Samoa), Tonga) were not pleased with this new state, so with the consent of **Australia** and **New Zealand**, Tongan troops occupied the reef. The situation re-occurred in 1982 when another attempt was made to declare independence. Today, Minerva Reefs remains an area of dispute between Fiji and Tonga, and there is still no sign of this tax-free nation.

Acknowledgements

Mapping

pp 14–22, 26–32, 38, 50, 130–136, 140–146, 152-156, cover, endpapers and all locator maps © Collins Bartholomew; pp 24, 36, 40–46, 52–126, 138, 150, 160–228 © MapTiler © OpenStreetMap contributors, plus bathymetry © GEBCO Compilation Group (2020).

Images

p6–7 © zelvan/Shutterstock; p12–13 © imageBROKER.com GmbH && Co. KG / Alamy; p34 © StevanZZ/Shutterstock; p35 © Alex Ramsay / Alamy; p42 © CC BY 3.0, https://commons.wikimedia.org/wiki/File:Flag_of_the_Kingdom_of_the_Two_Sicilies_(1816).svg ; p48 © imageBROKER.com GmbH && Co. KG / Alamy; p49 © footageclips/Shutterstock; p76 © CC BY_SA 3.0, https://commons.wikimedia.org/wiki/File:St._Blaise_-_State_Flag_of_the_Ragusan_Republic.svg ; p78 © kubek_77/Shutterstock; p79 © olrat/Shutterstock; p80 © CC BY_SA 3.0, https://commons.wikimedia.org/wiki/File:Blason_ville_fr_Saint-Malo.svg ; p88 © CC BY_SA 4.0, https://commons.wikimedia.org/wiki/File:Senarica_Flag_Reconstruction.svg ; p94 © Anna Krivitskaya/Shutterstock; p95 © CC BY_SA 4.0, https://commons.wikimedia.org/wiki/File:Piazza_della_Borsa_7_(IMG_20211010_081811).jpg ; p96 © CC BY_SA 3.0, https://commons.wikimedia.org/wiki/File:Free_Territory_Trieste_Flag.svg ; p100 © Alexandre.ROSA/Shutterstock; p104 © CC BY_SA 4.0, https://commons.wikimedia.org/wiki/File:Drapeau_Royaume_Ait_Abbas_(Beni_Abbès).svg ; p108 © CC BY_SA 3.0, https://commons.wikimedia.org/wiki/File:Flag_of_Klein_Vrystaat_-_2.svg ; p114 © CC BY_SA 4.0, https://commons.wikimedia.org/wiki/File:Flag_of_the_Republic_of_Salé_(1624-1668).svg ; p118 © mbrand85/Shutterstock; p119 © Jan Bures/Shutterstock; p126 © CC BY_SA 3.0, https://commons.wikimedia.org/wiki/File:Flag_of_the_Sultanate_of_Zanzibar_(1963).svg ; p128 © Olga S photography/Shutterstock; p134 © Lindasj22/Shutterstock; p135 © Ian Kennedy/Shutterstock; p142 © Darryl Brooks/Shutterstock; p143 © pablopicasso/Shutterstock; p148 © Chiara Magi/Shutterstock; p149 © CC BY_SA 4.0, https://en.wikipedia.org/wiki/File:Luther_Parker_stele_at_Pittsburg_town_park_2.jpg ; p158–159 © Wirestock Creators/Shutterstock; p164 © Nejdet Duzen/Shutterstock; p165 © asims_gallery/Shutterstock; p174 © CC BY_SA 3.0, https://commons.wikimedia.org/wiki/File:POL_COA_Gryf.svg ; p180 © Aaditya Chand/Shutterstock; p181 © Damira/Shutterstock; p188 © CC BY_SA 3.0, https://commons.wikimedia.org/wiki/File:Byzantine_imperial_flag,_14th_century.svg ; p194 © CC BY_SA 4.0, https://commons.wikimedia.org/wiki/File:Flag_of_the_State_of_Upper_Yafa.svg ; p196 © dec925 / Shutterstock; p198–199 © Lukas Bischoff Photograph/Shutterstock; p210 https://commons.wikimedia.org/wiki/File:Runit_Dome_001.jpg ; p211 Danita Delimont/Shutterstock; p222 © Granger/Shutterstock; p223 Photograph by and courtesy of Elena Pasilio, Nukunonu, Tokelau @tokelauelena; p230–231 © robertharding / Alamy Stock Photo.

A note from the author

I would like to thank my son Boris and my wife Danijela, who were my constant inspiration and whose smiles always removed the fatigue from a night of writing. I am also grateful to Nada Milosavljević for her fast and precise translations. Finally, my thanks to the entire team at HarperCollins Publishers, especially Harley Griffiths, Robin Scrimgeour, Julianna Dunn, Karen Marland, Craig Balfour and Jethro Lennox.